JOHNNY ANGEL

A Novel

By

Danny Falcone

MW01242018

Copyright © 2022 Daniel Falcone

All rights reserved. No part of this publication may be reproduced, distributed, or transmitted in any form or by any means, including photocopying, recording, or other electronic or mechanical methods, without the prior written permission of the publisher, except in the case of brief quotations embodied in critical reviews and certain other noncommercial uses permitted by copyright law.

ISBN: 978-1-957837-66-6

Contents

ACKNOWLEDGEMENT

The characters in this novel are purely fictional. If they resemble anyone, it is merely a coincidence.

To my children and grandchildren, I love you all… I'd also like to thank my editor Malory Wood of the Missing Link LLC

CHAPTER ONE

The three men left the restaurant laughing. It was a good meal and an enjoyable conversation—a nice way to start off the night. "Where you wanna go?" Frank Aganti asked. He was in a good mood and enjoyed being out with other made guys like himself. These were his true family, the people who really understood him. People he could trust.

"Let's go get some broads," replied Danny.

"Yeah, I know some hot young chicks from near my way," Nicky Black said. "Let's go by my place, and I'll have them come over."

"What about the wife and kids?" asked Danny? "Gone for the weekend."

"That sounds like a good plan to me," Frank agreed.

Danny drove the boy uptown to the Bronx. They joked the whole way. Traffic was light on the FDR Highway and slightly heavier on the Cross Bronx Expressway. When they reached Nicky's house, they entered through the garage. As Nick was unlocking the door, Danny came up behind Frank with a garrote and wrapped it around his neck. As Frank began choking, he lashed and bucked wildly. Nick quickly grabbed a hunting knife that was placed on the nearby garage shelf earlier that day. He plunged the knife deep into Frank's chest. After a few minutes, Frank's legs stopped twitching, and he lay still.

Danny released the garrote and let Frank's dead body hit the ground. "Damn," Danny said, "I was trying to save you all the bloody mess by choking his ass. Why did you start stabbing him?"

"You looked like you were having a hard time. I didn't want him to wear you out."

"Very funny. Now, look at this mess. We got to get this cleaned up before your wife comes home," Danny said, looking around for something to wipe his hands on. Both men were dressed in slacks and sport coats, neither wanting to ruin their clothes.

"Relax. She took the kids to her mom's for the weekend. What are we doing with him?" Nicky asked, nodding toward the lifeless body of Frank Aganti.

"Charlie and Bats are coming for him. They'll be here any minute. He's going into the old woodchipper."

Nicky shuddered at the thought. "Do me a favor, would you? If you ever have to whack me, don't do it that way."

"I'll take that same respect if you don't mind."

"That's a deal, pal." Both men knew in that this life, that was always a possibility.

A van backed into the driveway moments later. Two men quickly climbed out and checked the surroundings for any onlookers. Coast clear. Charles "Charlie Ponz" Ponzetta and Joseph "Joe Bats" Siccora immediately removed the body from the garage. Within ten minutes, they were finished moving the body and cleaning up. They got back in the van and pulled away.

Danny and Nick started the clean-up process. Daniel "Danny East" Tucci was a made member of the Genovese Family and part of the Harlem crew. He got his nickname being from the East Side of Manhattan. Danny was a valuable member—smart, tough, and all capable. He had a large crew of shooters under him.

Nicholas "Nicky Black" Tascomonni was also a made member of the same crew. Nick was strong and stocky, built like a bulldog. He had large, penetrating black eyes, hence the nickname. Nicky and Danny had grown up together and committed crimes with each other for the last thirty-five years. They started robbing candy stores when they were ten and had been involved with every aspect of illegal activity of some sort or the other ever since. Both men had grown up on the streets as real gangsters. Their reputations far exceeded them.

There was a third man, not with them at the moment. His name was Giovanni Bassemo, also known as "Johnny Angel." At forty-five years old, he still looked like he did at thirty. Five feet and ten inches tall and one hundred eighty-three pounds of mostly muscle, Johnny had dark black hair that still showed no sign of grey and a handsome face. Women loved him, and men feared him. The three men had been friends all their lives. Johnny just finishing up a five-year sentence in the state prison and was due out in three days. He couldn't wait to get out and reunite with his boys.

As soon as Nicky and Danny finished the clean-up that Charlie Ponz and Joe Bats started, they drove down the East Side Drive to 116th St. and Pleasant Ave. in Harlem.

In the late 19th and early 20th century, a huge wave of Italian immigrants moved to this part of Harlem, and it became known as Italian Harlem. Over the years, it had changed to mostly Latin immigrants and was now known as Spanish Harlem. There was still a small stubborn patch of Italians living there, but they mostly moved on. The Italian presence was still in social clubs, though, also their headquarters were. They needed to report to their capo Ralph "Ralphie Arms" Lamontino. Ralph, now in his late seventies, was a big man. His nickname came from his huge arms that once upon a time were all muscle. Now, they seemed more like fat than steel in the winter of his life.

When Danny and Nick arrived, Ralph emerged from the front door and met with the guys. They walked as they talked. "It's done," Danny said. "Ponz and Bats picked up the package."

Ralph nodded his head. "It's a shame, but what are you gonna do?" He was chewing on a toothpick and flicked it into the street. Nothing else had to be said about the unfortunate Franky.

To clear the silence, Nick piped up, "Johnny will be home Thursday. We're gonna throw a party for him Friday night at Nunzio's."

The old man smiled. Everyone knew that his favorite soldier was Johnny Angel. "God, I missed that son of a bitch," Ralph said, more to himself than Danny and Nick. "Danny, go see everyone in the crew and tell them I said to pass the hat for Johnny. We need to set him up good so he can relax for a while."

Danny shook his head. "No problem boss, but you really don't think the Angel is gonna relax for a while, do you?"

"No, but it'll be good to have him home."

"Yeah," Nicky agreed. "I miss the ugly bastard too." The three men all smiled, each with their own thoughts and memories of Johnny Angel.

Danny remembered back when they were kids, and all of a sudden, his memories overtook him. It was thirty some odd years ago… The snow was falling as the three young twelve-year-old kids ran up the block, each carrying a burlap sack full of dimes. They had spent the last five hours going through New York City, emptying the parking meters. When they robbed a car the night before, they found a set of keys and a badge from a city official. The burlap bags were heavy, and Nicky was complaining.

Johnny said, "You want me to carry that for you?"

"That would be sweet," Nicky replied.

"It wouldn't be sweet when I keep the money." An evil grin spread across Johnny's face.

Danny laughed and said, "I'll carry it and only charge you half the bag."

"You can both go and fuck yourselves," Nicky said and hefted the bag up in his arms.

"Yeah, I thought so," Johnny said. Their laughter could be heard down the next several blocks.

They stopped outside the Pleasant Avenue social club that belonged to the mob guys. Ralphie Arms pulled up in a new Cadillac at the curb as they reached the front door. He got out, and even though his winter coat, one could tell he was all muscle. He looked at the three neighborhood kids who stood in awe just mere feet away. They were good kids, but they were always up to something. Ralph liked the oldest one named Johnny. He showed prospects for the future. Ralph had his eye on him. "What are you kids up to now?" he asked in a menacing voice.

These three kids were no punks, yet they were always respectful. Ralph knew he was a scary figure to them, but Johnny never showed any fear—which is why Ralph liked him best. "We made a score," Johnny said, holding up his bag of coins.

"Come inside. It's too fucking cold out here." The boys looked at each other and did what they were told. They walked into the clubhouse, following Ralph inside. What a thrill to be entering the famous social club! If nothing else happened today, they would be happy just having entered the club of the neighborhood big shots. There were many guys playing cards and sitting around talking just inside the door.

Ralph looked at the bags and said, "You call that a score? What, did you knock over someone's piggy bank?" He had said it loud enough for everyone to hear. Laughter erupted—except from the three young boys.

Danny and Nicky's faces grew beet red in an instant. Johnny paid them no attention. He stayed focused on the goal. He wanted to impress Ralph. "Yeah, well, we have an endless supply of these piggy banks—and we're here to cut you in on it."

"There's no such thing as an endless supply of anything, Johnny. So, what gives?" Ralph asked, narrowing his eyes at the young buck.

Johnny dug into his pocket and pulled out the key. "We got the key to all the parking meters in the city."

The room grew quiet. Ralph was impressed. It was still small potatoes for him, but it was a nice little score for the kids. Plus, they could stick it to the city. He was intrigued. "And where'd you get that?" He leaned down to Johnny's eye level.

Johnny shrugged his shoulders and waved a hand aimlessly in the air. "Does Macy's tell Gimbels?" he asked.

Everyone in the room laughed, but Ralph kept a straight face; even though he was enjoying this game with the kids, he winked to one of his men standing there.

"Don't get smart with me, you little punk. I'll wipe the floor with you." He stood straight up again and looked down the tip of his nose at the boy.

"Geez, Ralph, I ain't trying to be smart. I just wanna dump this load so we can go get more." Johnny remained unphased.

"Take it to the bank. What do I look like, a fucking coin counting machine?"

"We can't go to the bank with this, Ralph. They'll get suspicious." Nick and Danny nodded their agreement.

"All right," he said, being generous. "Leave 'em here, and I'll give you a double sawbuck for each bag."

Danny and Nick were more than happy with that, but Johnny said, "Twenty dollars for a bag? There's probably a couple of hundred in each bag! That ain't fair."

Ralph had to bite his tongue to not laugh. He put on his best mad face and said, "Fair. You want fair? Go to the fucking bank." He pointed out the door. "You want money from me? It's twenty a bag; take it or leave it."

Johnny nodded his head and said, "You're right. Since we're with you and you're our boss, twenty each is okay." He crossed his arms over his chest to assert his young dominance.

"With me? Don't you go around saying you're with me just because you brought me a bag of fucking dimes If you were with me, you wouldn't be stealing change." Ralph reached into his pocket and pulled out a wad of bills that could choke a horse. He peeled off three twenties. "Here, now get the fuck out and don't get your asses caught robbing the city—and don't be telling people you're with me."

Danny and Nick nodded their heads nervously and said in unison, "Thank you."

Johnny simply smiled and said, "Thanks, boss." As they were walking out the front door, Ralph said, "Johnny, come back in an hour. I might have some real work for you. Come by yourself."

The memories were as real as if they happened yesterday. Danny laughed. "Hey, boss, you remember when we came to you with all the change from the parking meters when we were kids?"

The old man smiled. "Yeah. I haven't been able to get rid of you bastards ever since." Then the old man had thought. He smiled. "Before I give Johnny the envelope that you collect, I want you to get an old burlap bag full of dimes, and we'll give him that for his welcome home present."

The three gangsters stood out on the street and had a good laugh. That would be fun. They could not wait to see the face of their pal Johnny Angel when he saw his homecoming gift.

CHAPTER TWO

Russian Jews started coming to New York in the mid-seventies and settling in Brighton Beach, Brooklyn. In the eighties, after the fall of the Soviet Union, Russia allowed Jews to leave in a massive wave, and most continued their trek to the same corner of New York City's most populous borough. Among the many good people, there were bad ones like any other population. And among the bad ones, there were some really bad ones. Two of the very bad ones came to America one year apart. Vladimir "Vip" Pusnoski was a high-ranking member of The Solntsevskaya Bratva, one of the three Russian Mafia groups.

'Bratva' meant 'brotherhood,' and this organized crime group was one of the most powerful in the world. The second man was Boris "The Fighter" Alekseyev. He was the top man in The Izmaylovskaya Gang, which had brotherhoods set up in Tel Aviv, Berlin, Paris, Madrid, Toronto, Miami, and of course, New York City—with their stronghold in Brighton Beach. Boris quickly moved up the ranks and became the number one man in Brooklyn.

Though Vladimir's Bratva was more powerful, Boris and his gang were more deeply established in America. Boris had the protection of the Genovese Family, having made a friendship with Johnny Angel years ago. The tension between the two Russian brotherhoods had been heating up lately, and last week, one of Boris's men was found shot to death in his car. Boris was fuming and wanted answers. It was a professional hit done with a silencer. The victim was sitting behind the wheel of his car. Someone walked up to the window, no doubt someone he knew and trusted. Boris sat in the office of his moving company, contemplating the situation. His friend Johnny was getting out soon, and he hated the idea of a war between Brotherhoods at this time.

He wanted to show his Italian benefactor that he was running things smoothly—but he had to retaliate, or it would look like a sign of weakness. He called in his two most trusted men, Ivan and Maxim. "I want you to pick a low-level Solntsevskaya and execute him. I want it done today."

The men looked a little puzzled. "Who?" asked Ivan.

"What are you, an owl? Who who-who. I don't care who, just pick one and do him! What don't you understand about that?" His face began to turn beet red. He was feeling the pressure.

Maxim had been a loyal soldier for years and had killed many men but never on orders like this. 'Just pick one. He was unsure how to proceed, but he did not want to make Boris mad. He simply said, "No problem, Boris."

"Good. I want him shot in the head and use a silencer, understood?" Both men nodded yes and were dismissed. Boris sat and thought about everything happening at this point in his life. He was making so much money he did not know what to do with it all. His friend Johnny Angel would be able to help him with that. He wondered exactly when he was getting out, knowing it was any day now. He would throw a big party for him with booze and fine women, and then he would present Johnny Angel with a fat envelope. Men like Johnny were very rare, and he wanted him to understand how much he appreciated their friendship. He had put money on Johnny's books and sent many packages over the last five years. Their bond was strong and secure, which may very well be needed if he had to wage war on the Solntsevskaya.

***

Vladimir sat with ten of his men in their headquarters. "Why," he asked, "did we not get that deal for the stolen oil? How did that prick Boris wind up with it?" No one wanted to speak up, and that infuriated Vladimir even more. He slammed his fists on the long conference table. "So, what have we done about this?"

Finally, Mensk, his most trusted aide, spoke. "We have taken out the broker who made the deal as a warning for Boris not to interfere in the oil trade again."

That seemed to appease Vladimir somewhat. "Okay," he said in a softer voice. "We also need to make it clear on the other side that they should only trade with us. Send them the same message."

The third in command, Peter, asked, "Will that not piss them off and make them go against us for good?"

Vladimir shook his head and stared at him with a hard cold look. "Are you doubting me, Peter?"

"No, never, you know that. I am just trying to figure this out."

"A good soldier never questions his orders. Leave the figuring out to me, Peter, and we will continue to prosper. Our friends abroad must learn that when they cross us like this, someone will die."

Peter bowed his head and said, "Forgive me, Vip, I apologize."

Vladimir Pusnoski was a cold-blooded killer who ran his gang with an iron fist, yet sometimes he actually showed some human qualities. He smiled, stood up, walked behind Peter, and placed his hands on his shoulders. "Apology accepted, my friend. I know you are a loyal soldier, and we share this great Brotherhood together, as we all do. Let us not bicker anymore on mistakes but rather focus on our blessings. Where do we stand with the women from the Nigerians?"

Mensk spoke right away. It was much easier discussing good results than bad ones. "We have sealed a deal for twenty-five new girls. They will be delivered to Spain, where your brother Mika will take over."

Just then, there was a knock on the door, and a man entered. "Excuse me for interrupting, sir, but they have just found young Roman shot to death in his car."

Vladimir turned back to Mensk and sarcastically said, "It looks like Boris has replied to your warning."

CHAPTER THREE

The Triads were an old, organized crime group with their origins being in China. They started as resistance forces, opposing the Manchu rule in China during the Qing Dynasty in the early eighteenth century. Following the fall of the Qing Dynasty in 1911, the Triad themselves were disorganized and unmotivated to survive. The rebels were unable to return to their lives as ordinary citizens. They spent years as outlaws in grave danger and extreme violence. Many of them formed criminal organizations.

Today, there are many independent Triad groups with a similar organizational structure. The "Mountain Master," or "Dragon Head," is the leader and can also be identified by the number 489. The next tier of command is the "Vanguard" or "Operation Officer" along with "Deputy Mountain Master" and "Incense Master," who is the "Ceremonies Officer." All three positions can be identified by the number 438.

Next is the "White Paper Fan," "Administrator" number 415. Then is "Straw Sandal," who is "Liaison Officer" number 432. "Red Pole" is the "Enforcers" number 426.

Below them are the "Ordinary Members' number 49, followed by "Blue Lanterns, " not yet initiated members. This structure holds for all the different Triad groups.

An offspring of the Triad is the Tongs started in America in the second half of the nineteenth century. The Mountain Master is a man named Meng Chang, also known as Lee. Though his power reigned throughout the world, his base and strength were in Chinatown, New York City.

Lee is the CEO of Vigorous Enterprises Inc., a conglomerate of about thirty-five companies worldwide. The name "Meng" meant 'fierce' or 'vigorous'; hence the name of the company. Over the years, Lee took all the illegal money and invested in legitimate businesses, building a vast empire from the sweat and blood of the streets.

His Operations Officer, Cheng, kept a tight grip on the criminal enterprise along with the Deputy Mountain Master, Anguo, and the Liaison Officer, Cai. These three men, his most loyal, would meet with Lee regularly. Cheng expressed concerns about the Yakuza, the Japanese Mafia at today's meeting.

"Have they gained any ground here in Chinatown?" Lee asked.

Cheng shook his head. "No, not here, but elsewhere. Uptown and in Queens; they are taking over the gambling rooms. It's not like it used to be where the

Chinese play in one place, the Koreans in another, and the Japanese in their place. Now everyone plays together. It is crazy, but that's what is happening."

Lee sat down in a plush leather chair that sat behind his huge, handcrafted desk. And rubbed his chin. He did not care about the pennies Cheng spoke of, but it was more about honor and principles. They sat in his office in the lap of luxury, part of a company that made millions of dollars annually, worried over a few hundred dollars at a card game. The Yakuza was a violent lot of thugs, hard to talk to. It was worth trying to work out a suitable resolution before they started killing one another. He knew the Yakuza were hooked up with the Columbo family. He also knew his old, dear friend Johnny Angel would be of help. All the Mafia Families worked together these days, so that would not be a problem. Lee received word that Johnny was due home this week. He was looking forward to seeing his old friend. He would have a small party to honor his freedom and discuss this Yakuza problem.

Lee promised he would address the problem and then dismissed everyone. He sat for a few minutes and thought about his old friend Johnny Angel, and soon he was lost in memories. He went back to when he was thirteen years old and 24 locked up in The Bronx House of Detention. It was his first day there. He was sitting in the yard minding his own business when a group of about six boys started making fun of him, calling him Bruce

Lee. One kid kicked Lee's foot and told him to stand up. Lee stood up with his back to the wall. Obviously, he was about to get his ass kicked badly—until Johnny Angel showed up. Lee smiled, remembering the little, skinny, fearless kid from Harlem and what balls he had. Completely fearless.

He had never met Johnny before, but he stood in front of Lee and said, "He's my friend."

"Well, ain't that nice," the group leader said. He was twice the size of Johnny. "A Wop and a Chink; meatballs and fried rice." All the boys laughed, and then Johnny kicked him square in the balls, then quickly turned and punched the next kid right in the nose. Blood spurted all over, and everyone started fighting.

Lee laughed, remembering how they had given the six attackers hell. He could not remember if they actually won the fight, but he knew they did some damage. All the kids that were involved got locked down for five days. Lee and Johnny were in the same cell. Johnny had a fat lip and a black eye, but he did more damage to the others.

When they were alone, Lee said, "Thanks for helping. My name's Lee."

Johnny shook his hand and said, "They call me Johnny Angel. Nice to meet you, Lee. You fight pretty good. I was hoping you knew that karate shit but all the same, you did well."

"Why did you help me?" Lee had asked.

Johnny looked over at Lee and smiled. "You looked scared and like you could have used some help. Besides, I hate those Irish scumbags."

"Well, thanks again." "No problem. Maybe someday you'll return the favor." Lee smiled again. How could either of them know that fight would be the beginning of a great long friendship? They did eighteen months together, and Johnny got out three weeks before Lee. Three years went by before they saw each other again. Lee loved to tell the story of how Johnny and two other guys were hanging out in Little Italy one night, and they crossed over Canal Street and into Chinatown. They were a little drunk and looking for a lot of trouble. They started with some Tongs, and within minutes, they were surrounded by forty gang members. They were about to get in serious trouble when Lee showed up unbeknownst to Johnny. Lee had become the leader of the Tongs. He loved to tell anyone who would listen how he was Johnny's angel that night.

As the years went by, they had many deals and had many good times together. They made plenty of money as Johnny rose the ladder in the Italian Mafia, and Lee came to be Dragon Head of the Tongs. Johnny was family to Lee, and he could not wait to see him.

CHAPTER FOUR

Hector Lopez, a.k.a. "Yankee," sat on the hood of his car outside the corner bodega on 155th and 8th Ave in the tough Washington Heights neighborhood. He was the king there, and Washington Heights was his kingdom. Back in the 1960s, there was a famous player for the New York Yankees whose name was Hector Lopez, which is why this Hector Lopez got the nickname Yankee.

The June sun was stronger than usual on this beautiful afternoon. The corner had dozens of people hanging outside. First, Yankee congratulated his team for taking over first place. Then, he treated everyone, coaches and family members alike, to brunch at his restaurant. Yankee sponsored the neighborhood baseball team and hugely supported the urban baseball league. He was proud of how the kids played baseball, his favorite sport.

Many kids from the neighborhood had enough talent to play in the majors, but the streets ate them up before making it out. Manny Ramirez and a few others were fortunate enough to escape their environment and become true baseball legends. Unfortunately, most weren't so lucky. Next week, they would play the team from the South Bronx, and those kids were good—really good. The neighborhood bookie had his team a seven-six favorite. He gladly laid the seven and put up $2800 to win $2000.

He had already given his speech to the team and thanked the coaches and family members. He was waiting for Tito, his top lieutenant, to come out so they could go when Theresa came up to him. Yankee lit up when he saw her. "Ay Mamacita, how are you?"

Theresa kissed him hello and then turned to her ten-year-old daughter. "Say hello to Uncle Hector."

The little girl ran to his arms and hugged him. He was a father figure to her. She was Johnny Angel's daughter, but he'd been gone for half her life, so Yankee took over the role. She was his goddaughter, and Johnny was like a brother to him.

"How's my little angel?"

"Good, thank you," she replied.

Johnny made sure she was sent to private schools for a good education. She was a good kid and smart, all A's in school. Her name was Angela, but everyone called her Little Angel after her dad. She was looking more and more like her father every day. Yankee was amazed just looking at her.

"Hector," Theresa said, a little unsure of herself, "when will he be home?" Yankee looked at her, again seeing what a beautiful woman she was. Their relationship was like brother and sister, and that's what he always wanted it to be because of Johnny. He knew how much she was waiting for Johnny to come home. Five years of not dating, not because of the lack of want but because of Yankee's power and the fear he instilled in everyone. He had made it known that Theresa was his brother's woman, and she was off-limits.

He smiled when he answered, "tomorrow." She smiled too. She fought back the tears as she asked, "Will he come home to us?"

Yankee saw that one coming from the left field, yet he was unsure how to reply. "Who knows what an Angel will do? We'll have to wait and see, Theresa."

She figured he would answer her in his roundabout way, but she had to ask. "The place is already; it looks beautiful. Hector, I can't thank you enough."

They had been redoing many buildings in Spanish Harlem, and Hector bought a condo for her. They were all high-dollar plush condos, and he moved her into it two months ago. For the last five years, he had her in a decent place in this neighborhood where he could keep a better eye on them, but now he wanted her to settle in and have everything ready for Johnny should he choose to move in with her.

"No need to thank me, Theresa. You know only too well that if it weren't for Johnny, I would not be here today. He saved my life. I was supposed to die that night. No, I can never do enough for the three of you."

They chatted a few more minutes, and she kissed him goodbye, as did Angela. He promised to come by as soon as Johnny was out. While he watched them walk away, he thought about his friend Johnny Angel and that night when he cheated the Grim Reaper.

It was around ten at night, and they were partying on 79th Street between First and Second Avenues. It was a bar/restaurant, and they had the whole back tables taken. Johnny was in the kitchen snorting a few lines with Danny and Nicky when three guys came in with guns, grabbed Hector, and started dragging him out of the restaurant. As they reached the front door, Johnny came out of the kitchen and immediately pulled his pistol out, and ran after them. Just as they reached the middle of the street, Johnny opened fire on them. By this time, Danny and Nicky were there with guns blasting too. The kidnappers dropped Hector and ran for cover as they returned fire. In the middle of Manhattan, they had a Wild West shoot-out like the gunfight at the O.K. Corral. In the midst of bullets flying, Johnny ran out and grabbed Hector, and dragged him back to safety.

They busted in on Hector's cousin's apartment that same night in Queens. They shot and killed him, his wife, and kids, not touching the five kilos of cocaine and a half of a million in cash that was there. It was the beginning of a long war between cartels, and now years later, Hector's cartel was still in power, and the other one had been wiped out slowly but surely over time.

The next day, Hector sent a brand-new Cadillac to Johnny and gave him five kilos of cocaine. In those days, a kilo of coke cost about $65,000. Johnny split it with Danny and Nicky, but it was still good for everyone. Sitting there in his neighborhood on the hood of his car, Hector smiled at the thought of his dear friend coming home. He would throw him a big party with plenty of beautiful women.

He would not let Theresa know—but Johnny needed a party. He could not wait to see his old friend.

CHAPTER FIVE

From 125th Street, where the Apollo Theater stands up to 155th Street, Washington Heights begins as prime real estate for drugs, gambling, and prostitution. Mark Owens, a.k.a. "Apollo" made an undisputed claim of these forlorn blocks for the past twenty-five years.

The numbers game originated in Harlem and was still very popular there. So was shooting craps. All the crap games, poker games, and number spots belong to Apollo. There are specific blocks that sell crack cocaine, heroin, and marijuana, and these also belong to Apollo. He also had about twenty beautiful, classy girls who ran an escort service for him. Every one of the women wanted to work for Apollo; he never liked the idea of pimping. He justified his actions because he never forced his girls to work. If that's what they did and wanted to do under his protection, that's their business, their decision. Once a long time ago, some guy called him a pimp, and Apollo beat him to within an inch of his life. No one ever made that mistake again.

Over the years, many people had been hurt or murdered trying to lay claim to that desperate, valuable territory—and Apollo always came out on top. He had about sixty ferociously loyal soldiers, and he made sure they all shared equally in the proceeds. There was a fund set aside for anyone that got arrested and might need bail money or a lawyer. If one of his members went to prison, his family got his share. Each member was on the books with a legitimate job, providing benefits for him and his family. If there were a Forbes 500 list of all the criminal organizations worldwide, Apollo's would be top of the list for "Best Job Opportunity."

He even believed in retirement if anyone wanted it. Not one of his members has ever ratted on the organization, and over the years, only three went to prison for more than five years. The safest area to live in Harlem was within Apollo's territory. He protected business owners without charge. He never extorted a business owner in his area and was always there to help. If a store owner had a problem, they usually went to Apollo, and he handled it with no charge, except for reasonable expenses. He kept the street drug sales confined to eight different blocks, and even there, you would find a semblance of order. The police did not want to mess with him because anyone who took over would be much worse for the neighborhood. At least, for the most part, things were fairly predictable under Apollo's control.

He knew Johnny was coming home any day, and he wanted to do something nice for him. After all, it was Johnny's mentoring that made Apollo so successful. His territory stopped at 155th St due to the structure Johnny helped him form.

He sat at his desk looking over a housing development proposal, reflecting on his old friend Johnny. Johnny had made the gambling business in Harlem possible for him to take over and had hooked him up with Yankee on the other side of 155th St. Johnny had advised him many times over the past twenty years, and his wisdom had always been right on the money. There was no doubt in Apollo's mind that Johnny Angel was the sharpest guy he knew. They had met over twenty years ago in Attica state prison. They were as friendly as possible between a Black man and a white man while in prison. Once they were both out, they did some business together, and as the years went by, they became good friends.

Apollo counted on Johnny's counsel many times. When Johnny was booking sports, he only took cash bets, unlike any other bookie back in the old days. He was the only loan shark who would not lend money without collateral. All this was years ago, but those simple rules were the basis for Apollo's business structure. He followed Johnny's lead.

Apollo had taken a thousand dollars from everyone's pay this week as a tribute to Johnny. He locked the envelope with $60,000 in his safe, turned off the lights, and left his office. His two bodyguards were waiting in the outer office. Cecil and Ray were as loyal as any men you might find. They both thought of Apollo as a God—or at the very least a genius. Cecil had been

36

struggling lately with the thought of retiring. His roots were from Georgia, and he longed to go back and buy a nice piece of land and relax. He had been promising his wife now for years. He finally got the nerve to bring it up. "Boss, you know, I've been working for you for twenty years now."

Apollo stopped and looked at him, then looked at Ray and said, "Is he looking for a raise?" All three men cracked up laughing.

Cecil said, "No, boss, but I'm thinking about retiring."

Apollo stopped laughing, and so did Ray. "What are you going to do, Cecil? Go back to Georgia and grow fucking watermelons?" Apollo and Ray laughed again, but this time Cecil only smiled.

"That's not a bad idea, boss."

Apollo shook his head. "Well, Ray, make a note that we'll soon have a watermelon connection. We'll set up stands on every corner in Harlem." He clapped his hands and rubbed them together.

"Guys are already selling watermelons on the corners," Ray said as seriously as can be.

Apollo loved these guys, but neither of them had any brains. "Well then, kill those sons of bitches and take over their spots."

Ray and Cecil did not answer; they just stood there with blank looks on their faces.

"It's a joke," Apollo said, "just a joke." He rolled his eyes and threw his hands in the air. Then, Apollo made sure they understood because these two guys would kill the President if he told them to.

"So, what do you think, boss?"

"I think you're out of your mind, but if that's what you wanna do, you know I wish you only the best. We'll miss you. When are you going to go?" "I think next year, boss." "Oh, well then, let's not waste any more time talking about it now! Johnny Angel is coming home any day now. I want to have a big party for him. Ray, go down and make arrangements to use the Cotton Club next week. Spare no expense. My Angel is back." He was really looking forward to seeing Johnny. He sure did miss him.

CHAPTER SIX

It was a perfect day—but what day wouldn't be a perfect day when you're released from prison? The June sun sat in a cloudless sky of endless blue, and Johnny saw that as a good omen. "Not a cloud on the horizon." He walked out of the administration office of the prison to a stretch limo that was awaiting him just outside. Johnny slid nice and easily into the soft leather seat and smiled. He nodded his head and clapped his hands together. A suit was hanging up inside the limo; shirt, shoes, and socks. A fresh hot pizza was also waiting. Johnny made his favorite drink—vodka and seven. He bit into a slice of pizza, savoring the delicate crust and melted mozzarella. His eyes rolled up into his head as he chewed and tasted each morsel. He acknowledged the sweet, pungent pizza sauce with a hint of oregano. This common fast food seemed like the finest cuisine on Earth. Five years without pizza—pure torture! Johnny changed into his new clothing during the hour-long ride back to the city. It was a pleasant ride, and he reflected on all that he had to catch up on.

Johnny was a handsome man in his late forties. His youthful face belied life's experiences, and he always had a smile on. To Johnny, life was a big joke. Johnny was a throw-back to the fifties and sixties. He loved oldies music; doo-wop was still his favorite. Sinatra and Elvis were his idols. Once years ago, Johnny gave a guy a beating because the man said Elvis was gay. He called the guy a communist piece of shit as he beat him up.

As the limo approached the city, Johnny was unsure where to go first. He figured he'd stop at his mother's place in Yonkers and then shoot down to Pleasant Ave. to check in with his capo Ralphie Arms. He gave the driver directions to his mom's place. It was always a little weird being free after incarceration. His mother lived with his sister and her twelve-year-old son, his nephew Anthony. It was a big house, and there was plenty of room for Johnny. He had a room there that his mother never let anyone sleep in. It was perfectly untouched, encapsulated in time.

Anthony was shooting hoops in the driveway when the limo pulled up. When Johnny went away, he was only seven years old, so he did not remember him except for all the stories he heard about an infamous family member. But, the minute Johnny stepped out of the limo, Anthony knew who he was. As Johnny walked up to him, he just stared back at him.

"Little Anthony," Johnny said with a smile. "How are you, boy?"

"Hello, Uncle John." He just stood there in awe of the powerful presence of his Uncle Johnny Angel.

"Come," he said, putting his arm around Anthony. "Is your mom inside?"

"Yeah, her and grandma are cooking."

"Of course, they are," Johnny said with a laugh. "What else would they be doing?" Johnny approached the door and walked directly into the kitchen.

His mother looked up and screamed. "Oh my God, Johnny!" She ran into his arms, quickly followed by his sister Susan who had heard the commotion and damn near jumped over the couch to get to him from the other room.

"You look great, John," Susan said as she got her turn to hug him. She always called him John. "When did you get out?"

"about an hour ago. This is my first stop."

His mom put on a face and said, "So you're not staying. Already you have to run." Her hands immediately went onto her hips as she popped one out.

Johnny flashed one of his famous smiles and said, "Relax, Mom. This was my first stop. That should make you happy. You know I gotta go downtown—but I'll be around now. I'm home."

They talked, laughed, cried, and ate. Tina Bassemo was so proud her son was home. She fed him until he begged for a break. Suddenly, after what felt like endless meals, he was tired and wanted to nap. Johnny stretched out on the couch and fell fast asleep. When he awakened, it was dark outside. He sat up, stretched, and walked into the kitchen. The limo driver was seated at the kitchen table, and Tina was feeding him.

He jumped to his feet when Johnny walked in and said, "Excuse me, sir, but your mom insisted I come in and eat. Are you ready to go now?"

"Yes, but finish your macaroni first. Then we'll go downtown."

   ***

Nick and Danny played knock rummy, $100 a game, $10 a point. Nick knocked after the second pick, caught Danny with about fifty points, and won the game. Danny threw the cards and cursed. "You lucky bastard! That's the only way you can win with a no-brainer."

Nick smiled and totaled the payoff. "I don't care what you call it or how I win. The only thing that matters is when the game is over, who pockets the money. You owe me $570." Danny was counting out the money when Johnny walked in.

"Is he still whooping your butt at gin?"

Nicky and Danny lit up with genuine smiles. They both jumped up to greet Johnny. Everyone else in the club noticed the presence in the room and the energy shift and quickly came over too. Ralphie was gone for the day already, but Nick told him they were having a dinner party tomorrow night in his honor, just their "Crew," their regime only. So they went outside and did the walk talk.

Danny said, "So what's up, pal? Where are you gonna be staying?"

"I'm not sure yet. Right now, I stopped by my mom's, and I'll just lay there for a while. It feels a little weird being home."

The three friends talked for almost an hour. Nick and Danny filled Johnny in on all the happenings over the last five years.

Danny said, "Me and Nicky went over every once in a while to give money to Theresa for Angela, but we knew Yankee was taking care of them, so we didn't go a lot."

"No, that's fine. I need to go by there now. What time you wanna get together tomorrow?"

"One last thing Johnny… We never got a lead on Uncle Lenny. He went into the Witness Protection Program and never showed his face again. He's got a new identity and over $3 million in cash. He took that whole crew down and robbed their money."

Johnny shook his head. "That piece of shit. You think he's still alive?"

"Don't know," Nicky answered, "but since he's your uncle, they came around asking for help. Wasn't much we could do—but he hurt a lot of friends of ours."

"Lenny has been with that crew for thirty years and knows that there's a problem. They wanna say he's my uncle. I asked my mom about him a couple of hours ago. She said that he calls from a private number every once in a while. Now that I'm home, I'll see what I can find out. He couldn't have spent the money. He's like eighty-five now. What's he gonna do with that kind of money?"

Nicky laughed. "Well, we'll just have to relieve him of the extra cash he doesn't need."

"Yeah," Johnny said, "and all the extra air he's breathing."

Danny laughed and said, "Watch out! Johnny Angel is back!"

***

The Polo Grounds was a bar on 8th Avenue that Hector owned. So what if nobody under the age of fifty had the slightest idea what The Polo Grounds meant or that the New York Giants once called it home. Willie Mays, the greatest ballplayer in history, played there—but that was another day, yesteryear. His bar would remain a tribute, a testimony to baseball as long as he was breathing, maybe even after he was gone.

His office was in the back room, and that was where he spent most of his time. Washington Heights was the neighborhood where the original Polo Grounds stood, and Hector, the great baseball fan, named his bar accordingly. Anyone could walk into the bar, but the last couple of tables in the back were for Hector's men, and no one could walk past them. So when Johnny walked into the bar, he headed straight for the back. He was stopped right away.

Johnny was not offended by the big man who stopped him. He knew the guy was just doing his job. "Tell Yankee he's got a visitor," Johnny said with a pleasant attitude.

"There's no Yankee here, my man. You're in the wrong place. Try uptown or somewhere else, carbon." Johnny looked to each side and laughed at how quickly Hector's guys surrounded him.

He pointed his finger at the man in front of him and said, "You see, we were just having a nice conversation, and you start with the name-calling." Johnny shook his head. "I'm gonna tell you this one more time, CABRON. Go tell Yankee he's got a visitor, or I will personally put you in the fucking hospital!" Johnny stared the man straight in the eyes. The young thug saw nothing but coldness in Johnny Angel's eyes.

"Wait here," he said and walked off to the back room. A minute later, Hector emerged. When he saw Johnny, he shouted, "Oh my God, Johnny!" The two men embraced, and everyone relaxed. Hector turned to his men and said, "This is the great Johnny Angel, my brother." They all knew of Johnny Angel, but none had met him before. They all knew the stories Hector always told.

The man who had stopped Johnny came over with his hand extended. "Please forgive me," he said. "I didn't know who you were."

Johnny smiled and shook the young thug's hand. "No problem, son. I like the way you did your job."

The big man smiled, and he felt O.K. again. Yankee yelled to the bartender, "Bring us a bottle of vodka and give everyone a drink on the house. Johnny Angel is home!" They sat at the back table, and each of the men came over to show their respect. Johnny Angel was a legend, and they were full of admiration for his presence.

Johnny reached over and put his hand on top of Yankee's hand. "My friend, I thank you for all you've done while I was away." Yankee seemed insulted. He waved his hand at Johnny.

"Like you wouldn't have done the same for me?"

"Nonetheless, my heart needed to tell you that."

"Ah, Johnny, it's so good to have you back. Wait till you see Angela. She is so beautiful." He held up a finger for emphasis, "—and Theresa has been faithful all this time."

"I don't know about all that, Hector."

"I do," he said quite seriously. "I've had her under close supervision. Yeah, maybe she snuck a piece here and there but never a man around the child. I would never allow that."

Johnny laughed. "You are a piece of work, my friend." He started looking around the place and then noticed Mombo, Hector's right-hand man, was not there. "Where's Mombo?"

Hector laughed. "Ah, Mombo got a promotion. He's in charge of all European distribution now. He will be happy to hear you are home." Then as an afterthought, he said, "Oh, I have something for you." Yankee got up from the table and disappeared inside his office. He opened the safe and took out an envelope. Coming back to the table, he handed it to Johnny. "A welcome home present."

Johnny took the envelope and slid it inside his jacket's inner pocket. "Thank you."

Hector waved his hand again. "What are your plans?"

Johnny shrugged his shoulders. "Who knows? I'll figure that out in a few weeks."

"I hope you'll consider staying with Theresa. I just moved her to a beautiful new condo in Spanish Harlem, top of the line. It would be good to have Angela get to know you."

"O.K., Daddy." Johnny laughed.

Hector laughed too. "I guess I sound like that, huh? O.K., I said all I will say about that."

"Take me over there, would you?"

Yankee laughed a good strong laugh. "I'd thought you'd never ask."

***

Spanish Harlem, also known as "El Barrio," goes from 5th Avenue to the East River and 96th Street up to 142nd Street. Spanish Harlem has the biggest Puerto Rican population in the world outside of Puerto Rico. Hector moved Theresa here because she was Puerto Rican and very close to Johnny's headquarters on Pleasant Avenue. The six-story brownstone had been completely renovated and filled with high-priced condos. Theresa lived on the top floor. As they entered the building, the doorman stopped them and said he needed to call up and announce them. Hector gave him a fifty-dollar bill and told him to take a walk. Then, leaving his bodyguards down in the lobby, he went upstairs with Johnny. When the elevator opened on the sixth floor, Hector said, "It's apartment B. Enjoy. I'll talk with you later."

The two men hugged, and Johnny walked slowly toward apartment B. Not sure of what he was feeling, Johnny almost turned around and left but instead, he forced himself to knock on the door. He heard a television inside and someone walking to the door. When it opened, he was face to face with Theresa for the first time in five years. Theresa had tried to visit Johnny, but he would not allow it. He did not want his daughter brought up there, and he insisted that Theresa move on with her life. She begrudgingly respected his wishes but sent a letter every week and many pictures over the years. She also spent every other weekend in Yonkers with Johnny's family so Angela could know that part of her family. Finally, she looked at Johnny and broke out in tears. Slowly, she approached him, and when he opened his arms, she embraced him. Her body racked with sobs as she cuddled against him.

"Are you gonna invite me in or what?" Johnny asked to break the awkwardness. She stepped aside, and Johnny entered. He looked around. "It's beautiful."

"Yes, it is," she agreed. "I've missed you so much," she said as she came to him and kissed his lips once more. Johnny grabbed her tightly and kissed her neck and her breast. Then, he picked her up and carried her to the bedroom. Five years of being locked away had him pent up with lust. In minutes, he exploded. He lay back, and Theresa put her lips all over him until he was once again hard. Then she climbed on top. They made love for what seemed like hours, and afterward, Johnny drifted off into a deep sleep.

She lay beside him, watching him, thoughts flooding her mind. She wanted to say so many things, but Johnny was not the type of guy you could manipulate or corner. He was a wild, free spirit, which was one of the things she loved about him. Despite her desires, she knew she had to let him alone. She could only hope he would make this his home. She spooned up against him and thought when he saw Angel; he would surely stay. She fell asleep with a smile.

CHAPTER SEVEN

Vladimir was furious. He had enough of this Boris, and it was time to set matters straight. Brighton Beach was not big enough for both of them. Boris had been a thorn in his side for far too long now. He had a missile launcher that he would like to shoot right into the nest of Boris and his whole crew, killing each and every one of them. He might get away with that in Russia but not here in America. The police would destroy the Brotherhood if he went that far. But that would bring too much heat from the Feds. He also knew doing something like that would be his own demise. No, he had to find a way to take Boris out and keep himself safe in the process. This had to be done the old-fashioned gangster way.

He called his Brotherhood in and declared war on the Izmaylovskaya Gang. "Our goal is to wipe them out, once and for all. Anyone who brings me Boris's head gets a $20,000 bonus. Send the troops out—and any of that gang out and about is open game. I don't want any bombs or any civilians getting hurt. As long as the police see this as a personal housecleaning, they will not respond too heavily—but if any innocent people get hurt, they will come down hard on us. Be careful."

When all the men left, Vladimir sat down in his chair and thought about a future without the

Izmaylovskaya Gang. He smiled at the thought. He looked forward to sending flowers to Boris's funeral.

***

George Zepcanchoiritz was a mole in the Solntsevskaya Bratva. He was placed there by Boris six years ago on the recommendation of Johnny Angel. As he was known on the streets, Georgie Z had turned out to be an untold wealth of information that Boris used to his advantage, prospering many times over. Georgie Z had turned Boris on to the stolen oil deal, reaping millions of dollars in profits for his boss.

When Boris's phone rang and saw that it was Georgie, he answered with a warm hello. "Georgie, my friend, how are you?" "I am fine, sir, but there is a problem." When Boris hung up with Georgie, he summoned all his people. His office was in a warehouse in his neighborhood, so that he would wait there for them. As he waited for everyone to gather, he contemplated the situation. He was not upset that Vip wanted war. This was part of the deal, part of the work he did. Instead, he looked at it as an occupational hazard, like a coal miner or cop; each job came with risk. People sometimes get killed. The problem was the timing—the timing was not good. He did not want Johnny Angel walking into any crazy rub-out attempt.

He would send word that he and Johnny should meet somewhere else. When everyone arrived, he explained the problem and immediately started making counter-offensive plans. Many of the Brotherhood on both sides were ex-military with training from the old branch of the Russian Special Forces; most combat veterans from Russian misadventures in Chechnya and Afghanistan. These were tough men, used to taking orders and used to taking chances.

Boris turned to Stephan Elson, son of Monya Elson, the most feared killer in the Russian Mafia. "Stephan, you take Vip. The quicker we can take him out, the quicker this war will end. I have a reliable source that might be able to tell us where Vip will be laying low. As soon as I hear something, I will let you know, but in the meantime, you start working it from your end."

Addressing everyone else, he said, "When you leave here, do not go home. Each of you should call your family and tell them you will be away for a while. Your team leaders have safe houses for all of you. Maxim and Ivan will stay with me. Dex, you will take a team and go directly to Vip's headquarters and kill anyone in sight. Good chance Vip is still there. If we get lucky and catch him there, we can end this war before it has even started. Either way, we will strike first, and they will be confused, and in that confusion, they will make mistakes. We will be there to take advantage of any and all of their mistakes."

Boris pumped his fist in a victory sign. War always excited him. They discussed plans a little further. All the men were ready for the hunt, having done this sort of thing more than a few times before. Finally, Boris said, "Everyone leaves through the basement. You'll come out on the next block. Go in small groups, move out together. O.K., guys, happy hunting." And with that, he slapped his hands together. The meeting was over.

When everyone was gone, Boris called his wife and told her he wouldn't be home because he had to leave town for a week or so. He told her to take the kids to her sisters and stay there until he told her to return home. With that out of the way, he called Danny East. "Hello, my friend. I was wondering if the Angel has landed yet?"

"Hey Boris, how are you? Yes, he landed yesterday."

"Ah, great, I'd love to see him…but coming here is not a good idea. Can you arrange something there in the city?"

"Yeah, I'll take care of it and call you later."

"Thank you, Danny. Talk to you later." Now that those two things were done, he turned to Maxim and Ivan. "Let's go to Atlantic City. If we need to get out of the way, at least let's have some fun."

***

Vip was planning to lay low for a while and was ready to go. He wished he could be part of the hit squads, but now his main concern was to have a good alibi. He would have enjoyed looking Boris in the eyes as his life left him. Too bad he was the boss and had a responsibility to his men. Sometimes being the boss meant missing all the fun. He called Mensk and Peter into the office. "I am leaving you two in charge. I will be in touch. Let's hit them hard. If we can take a bunch of them out before they even realize there's a war, we'll be way ahead of the game. Who is assigned to me?"

"We have four top soldiers waiting for you, Vip. They are all good men. They will stay with you until this is over."

"Good, then have them bring the car around. We will leave now before the shit hits the fan." Vladimir opened his desk drawer and pulled out a .380 automatic pistol. He checked to see if one was in the chamber and then put the safety on. Then, tucking the gun in his waistband in the small of his back, he clapped his hands and headed downstairs. The next few days would be very interesting indeed.

Dex sat across the street and watched as two men came out. One went to a parked car and brought it to the front. Dex spoke into a walkie-talkie, "Everyone to post, he's coming out." Eight men were stationed all around the building, easily blending in with the usual busy pedestrian traffic. Vip came out with two more guys behind him, and the hit team moved in. Dex had assigned two men to strictly take out Vip and the others to focus on the bodyguards. They did not waste any time or shots on the wild shoot-out when the team moved in. Each man had a specific target, and the hail of gunfire that followed was quick and precise. Vip and his men never got a shot off, and all five of them were down. One of the shooters walked up to Vip and shot him twice in the head—insurance shots. The whole incident lasted less than two minutes, and then they were gone. Mensk and Peter came running out with guns ready, but there was not anyone there except their dead comrades. They quickly disappeared.

***

Boris was in a limo driving to Atlantic City. He had many things on his mind, but the most pressing was that piece of shit, Vip. He wished he could have been there to kill him. Unfortunately, he had only been gone about an hour when the call came. He turned to his two most trusted men and said, "It is over already. Vip is dead, and so are all his bodyguards."

Maxim said, "We still need to lay low until we see what they will do. Peter and Mensk will be out for blood."

"Peter and Mensk are two fools. They will do as I tell them to do from now on, or they can join their boss. Send word to them that we want a sitdown with them. Assure them that they are safe. Give them a hostage to hold if you must but get them to the table."

"I know Mensk many years, boss, and he won't be easy to turn around."

"If they insist on a hostage, have someone follow them so we can get our man back. Then we'll kill Peter and Mensk too." Boris declared.

"What about the Italians? They won't like the fact that we've taken over and cut them out." Ivan said with no real concern.

Boris waved his hand and said, "The Italians are weak these days. I'll let Johnny Angel take care of them. Our Brotherhood has just doubled in size." All three men had a good laugh. Then, the phone rang, and Boris answered, "Yes? Ah, Danny, what's up?"

"Wednesday, two o'clock, Katz's deli," Danny said.

"Great, I'll be there. So long." Boris smiled a wicked smile and said, "Things just keep getting better. I think I'm gonna win big in Atlantic City, and Wednesday, I'm having lunch with an angel.

CHAPTER EIGHT

Peter and Mensk went straight to a safe house they had. "Well, what do we do now?" Peter asked.

"I must call Spain and tell Mika." This was out of their hand. They needed help, and Mika needed to know his brother was dead as soon as possible. He took out his phone and dialed the number. It was two in the morning there, but this could not wait. Strangely enough, Mika answered on the second ring.

"This should be very important," he said, devoid of pleasantries like 'hello' and 'how are you?'

"It is," Mensk replied. "Vip is dead. We are at war." The receiver was silent for an extended minute, and then Mika said, "I am on my way." And the line went dead.

"What is our next move? Mensk, you are the leader now. I think we must retaliate."

"We will wait for Mika to show up, and then we will plan our next move. For now, we stay put."

Peter had a worried look on his face.

"So, what are you thinking? You look like a lost puppy," Mensk asked.

"I think we need to get word to the troops that we are alive and okay. If they do not hear from us, they will fold to the Izmaylovskaya Gang."

Mensk thought for a moment and nodded his head. "Okay, call Georgie Z and have him come by here, and we will brief him. Let him tell the others."

While they were waiting for Georgie not long after, a call came from Mika. "I will arrive in JFK at noon tomorrow. Have someone there to get me."

A half an hour later, Georgie arrived at the safe house. The three men sat down and talked. George noticed the concern on their faces and their scared little fidgeting. These two were already defeated and trying hard to keep themselves from falling apart. He felt bad for them. After all, they weren't bad guys. "Boris is spreading the word that he wants to talk with you guys. I think that might be a good idea."

"Yeah, great idea," Mensk said sarcastically. "Why don't you run over there and talk with them. Why not tell them it's okay that they killed our boss and four of our brothers. Then we can all kiss and make up."

"I was just thinking it can't hurt to hear what they have to say."

"They'll say bang bang. You're dead."

"No," Georgie said as he nodded his head. "We insist on holding a hostage until you get back this way. It guarantees your safety."

"I will go," Peter said, "and hear what they have to say." George was trying to think fast. He did not want only one of them to go; that would complicate everything.

"If you want, I will go with you. You should not go alone."

"Georgie is right, Peter. You should not go alone," Mensk said. "We will both go. Okay, Georgie, set up a meeting tonight in a public place. Tomorrow when Mika arrives, we will discuss their terms."

"Ah, Mika is coming. Very good," George said, trying to get all the details.

"Yes," Mensk said. "You will be at JFK tomorrow noon to pick him up and bring him here at once."

"Okay," George replied. "Let me see if I can set up a meeting. I will go to Boris's warehouse, and if I am not back in an hour, then it was a set-up, and I will be dead." He tried keeping a somber look, but he really did not mean it because he knew none of this was real since he really was Boris's guy.

As George was leaving, Peter said, "Be safe, brother."

When Georgie left, Mensk turned to Peter and said, "As soon as Boris shows his face at the meeting, we start shooting. We hit Boris and whoever we can. We might not make it out of there, but at least we will have avenged Vladimir, and Boris will be dead."

"Won't they frisk us for weapons before we see Boris?"

"They should not. We are there to make peace, but just in case, we will hand over a pistol and have a backup one.

***

The Brighton Beach Café was a big coffee house owned by one of the Izmaylovskaya Gangs. It was a popular hang-out for the preppie college crowd. The back rooms, however, were for gang members and friends of the family. No strangers were allowed, ever. The meeting was set for five o'clock, but Mensk wanted to be there by four-thirty. Georgie left ten minutes earlier to pick up the make-believe hostage who would stay with him until the meeting was over. Of course, he was not going to pick anyone up because he knew what was going to happen.

Mensk and Peter left the building with many things on their minds—but never suspecting a double-cross. As they walked to the car, a hit team came out from all sides. The bullets tore through the number two and three men of the Solntsevskaya Bratva. There are many things one may think of when the moment of death finally comes; family, friends, a happy time, a loved one—but for Mensk, his last thought on Earth was, Oh shit. I fucked up.

Boris was on a good winning streak in Atlantic City. He was up about fifty thousand, and it seemed he could do no wrong. He just made fourteen passes on the Baccarat table while he had the shoe. When his phone rang, he stepped away from the table and said, "Yes?"

Georgie was calling from Brooklyn. "Three of a kind is always a good hand. Remember that while you gamble."

"Ah, thank you, my friend. I will hold that thought dear to my heart. What I'd really like to hear is four of a kind. Maybe I'll get lucky like that tomorrow. Good night." He stepped back to the table and turned to Ivan and Maxim. He leaned close and said under his breath, "Three down and one to go. Tomorrow at noon, Georgie will pick up the fourth ace. I hope he enjoys his ride to Brooklyn. We'll leave in the afternoon so there can be no doubt about where we were. I wish I could personally greet Mika tomorrow, but that just isn't a good idea. I can live with that. Too bad he can't." They all laughed and continued their game.

At 12:15 p.m. the next day, Mika stepped off the plane, and forty minutes later, he was through customs and sitting comfortably in the car with Georgie, headed for Brooklyn. "Tell me everything," he said as he crossed his legs. Georgie started from the stolen oil and brought him up to date.

"Where are Peter and Mensk now?" he asked. "They are waiting for you so we can decide what to do next. If it's okay with you, they said to go there right away."

"Yes. I'll need a car and a weapon before I go anywhere, so take me to the meet." They drove on in silence, Mika full of hatred, wanting revenge for the cold-blooded assassination of his brother. If he was sure of anything, he was sure he would taste their blood. Now that he was there, things were going to get bloody. When they got to Brooklyn, Georgie drove to an underground parking garage beneath an apartment building.

He turned to Mika and said, "They're on the fourth floor." As soon as he stopped and put the car into park, two men stepped up and opened fire on Mika with silenced pistols. Georgie got out of the way just in time as Mika took six rounds to the chest and then two to the head.

Georgie reached back in and wiped down the steering wheel and door panel with a hanky. All three men left together, leaving the car and the bloody body of Mika behind for the world to see. That afternoon, Georgie called a meeting with the entire Solntsevskaya Bratva and declared the conflict over and that he was now in charge of the Solntsevskaya Bratva in New York. No one knew that he was actually a plant or spy for Boris, though they did understand that they would be giving a small percentage over to him. As far as they were concerned, they were thankful to Georgie for protecting all the rackets they worked hard at. He was a hero in their eyes because usually, the spoils of war go to the victor. Maybe Boris was not such a bad guy after all. They had no problem abiding by the peace Georgie made. It kept money in their pockets, and it kept them alive to fight, steal and kill another day. Not a bad deal.

CHAPTER NINE

Apollo was smoking a big fat Cuban cigar when his secretary called and said there was a visitor to see him named Mr. Sanchez. Cecil and Ray frisked Sanchez before allowing him to enter the office. He walked into the office and meekly spoke. "Thank you for seeing me, Mr. Apollo."

Apollo had an open-door policy for the neighborhood people and was always being invited to weddings, baptisms, and every other special occasion. Most people recognized Apollo as the local Godfather. He took care of the merchants and citizens and shopped in all their local stores. They always tried giving him things for free, but Apollo insisted on paying. "Give me a discount, but you have to charge me," is what he told everyone.

"What is it you'd like to see me about Mr. Sanchez?"

"I own the big discount store on 124th Street."

"I know who you are, Mr. Sanchez. My question is, what do you want?"

"Your help, sir. I speak for all on our block. We want you to include us in your area of protection. It is only one more block for you." Apollo frowned. He wished he had a dollar for every time the merchants tried to get him to extend his boundaries.

All the surrounding areas were infested with wannabe gangsters and gangbangers. It took years to establish his kingdom and many wars to protect it. There was always some punk that crossed the line, and Apollo had to get rid of him. Lately, things have been nice and quiet, and all was well.

He could not risk the understanding he had with all the street people, especially since they were abiding by the rules. "I wish I could help, but I have established boundaries that I cannot cross. Unfortunately, you fall outside those parameters."

The man looked devastated at his response. "Mr. Apollo, they have struck my wife and put their filthy hands on my sixteen-year-old daughter. I beg you to protect us too." He was pleading at this point.

There was a quick moment of silence before Apollo answered, "Call the police and press charges on those thugs—but I cannot help you. I'm sorry." The look of fear and desperation in Sanchez's eyes touched Apollo, but he could not interfere. After a minute of personal deliberation, Apollo continued, "We are building some new storefront property on 127th Street. There is already a waiting list, but perhaps we can move you to the top of the list if you're interested. The rent is high dollar."

"Yes, but to be in your beautiful area is well worth it. Once you cross the street into your area, it is like entering a new world. You are a man that is much respected, Mr. Apollo. When will those spots be available?" His desperate face had a new glimmer of hope.

"Not long, maybe forty-five to sixty days. Ray will take you down to see the property manager and get you signed up. Sorry for your troubles, Mr. Sanchez."

Ray took Sanchez down the block and had him put on the top of the list. On his way back, as he was about to enter the building, Johnny Angel came up behind him. He put his finger in the small of Ray's back and said, "All right, just keep walking," Johnny said in a disguised voice. In one swift move, Ray's left arm came down and knocked Johnny's arm to the side. Spinning on one heel, he turned and kicked Johnny in the chest, sending him flying a few feet and falling on his butt. Ray was in attack mode when he finally saw that it was Johnny who was sitting on the sidewalk, laughing like a crazy man.

"Oh my God, Johnny," Ray said, running to help him up. "You crazy son-of-a-bitch! What's wrong with you! Man…I'm sorry, I didn't realize it was a joke." He was half-angry, half-relieved to see that Johnny Angel was okay and was there, free from prison.

Johnny grabbed Ray's outstretched hand. Still laughing, he said, "I see you're staying sharp. That's good, Ray, that's really good." He stood up and dusted himself off.

Ray kept apologizing. "Johnny, I'm sorry, I don't know what to say. Please forgive me." Johnny could not stop laughing. To him, it was all in jest.

"No problem, Ray, don't sweat it; it serves me right. I was fucking with you, and that's what I get. I don't know why I thought I could get the drop on you. I don't know what I was thinking there."

Ray was brushing Johnny off. He said, "Apollo is gonna kill me when he hears about this. It's good to have you back, Johnny Angel. You're just as crazy as ever."

"Is the boss man upstairs?"

"Yeah, does he know you're here?"

"No, I thought I'd surprise him—but not like I surprised you. Where's your sidekick?"

"He's with Apollo upstairs. Let me tell him some story to get him to come out so you can surprise him. You wait in the waiting room when we go up, and I'll tell him something to get him out there." When they got upstairs, Ray went into the office where Cecil was still talking about Georgia, and Apollo was still joking about watermelons.

"Hey, guys," Ray said with a serious face, "we got a problem with this nut job in the waiting room. We need to kick his ass out."

"Who?" Apollo asked.

"Some wise-ass gang banger," Ray said to keep the story going. Apollo reached in the desk drawer and pulled out an automatic pistol. He got up and tucked it into his waist. "What, are you getting too old to handle some punk kid?" They walked into the waiting room, Apollo ready to handle some punk kid.

Johnny said, "Is this the kind of welcome I get?"

"Johnny!" Apollo lit up. "Fucking Ray," he said as he punched Ray's shoulder playfully and hugged Johnny. They went back into the office, and Apollo broke out a twenty-year-old bottle of vodka. "I've been saving this for two years now, waiting for you to come home before I opened it." He got four glasses and poured everyone a drink. "First, we drink to our dear friend Johnny Angel, home safe and sound. Salute."

They all tapped their glasses and drank down the shot. The next round was already poured. "Next," Apollo began, "Johnny, you've come home just in time to get in on our new business. Cecil here is going back to Georgia to grow watermelons, and we're gonna take over the watermelon market on every street corner."

They all laughed, touched glasses, and downed their shots. After a few minutes, Cecil and Ray left the two old friends alone to catch up on things. Once they were alone, Apollo went into the safe and took out an envelope which he gave to Johnny. "A coming home present."

Johnny nodded his acceptance of the cash gift and thanked Apollo. It was an act of respect and friendship, and to refuse it would be disrespectful.

"What are your plans?" Apollo asked.

"Who knows? Don't really have any, not yet anyway. Just trying to get acclimated again. You got anything good going on?" Johnny sat in one of the plush chairs, and Apollo followed suit.

Apollo laughed. "Have you ever known me not to? I'm buying all the property I can and converting the buildings to condos. I'll let you buy in at cost. I think two hundred and fifty G's should get you about twenty percent. At the end of the day, when all is said and done, you should bring back a couple of million on your end."

Johnny smiled. "Good. Count me in. I'll bring you the money next week. Put it under the name of 'Johnny B. Good LLC'. It's a clean company." Johnny took the envelope Apollo just gave him and said, "How much is in here?"

"Sixty G's," replied Apollo. "That's very generous, thank you." Johnny tossed the envelope back to Apollo.

"Here's my down payment."

"Duly noted," Apollo said, catching the envelope. "Johnny, there's something you can help me with. There's this crew of Italian guys. I'm not quite sure what the deal is, but they're like a new kind of mafia. They have some good heroin at really good prices. You know I've been doing business with Lee for years now, ever since you hooked us up, but this product is supposed to be the best. What do you know about this?"

"You're referring to 'Camorra,' The Neapolitan Mafia. They're not new. They've been around longer than the Sicilian Mafia." Johnny did not bother to tell Apollo that all the guys in his crew headed by Ralphie Arms were Neapolitan and had close ties with Camorra, even though they belonged to the traditional Sicilian mafia family. In the last few years, the Camorra was breaking into America in a much stronger way, establishing gambling, loansharking—but mostly drugs. "How did you come across them?"

"Danny told me about it but said I'd have to talk with you before he introduced them. What do you think?"

"I don't have anything against them, but I wonder why you wanna fix something that ain't broken? You've got a good thing going on with Lee and Yankee. Why bring someone new into this? We're getting old, Apollo; we have a strong bond, a long history. Why take a chance on a new involvement?"

Apollo nodded his head. He had been waiting to see what Johnny thought, and he respected Johnny's opinion. That was all he needed to hear. "Okay, that's the end of that."

Johnny was a little upset though he did not show it. The fact that Danny mentioned it to Apollo meant that Danny was involved with the Camorra directly. Johnny wondered if Ralphie knew about this. He would definitely have a talk with Danny today. "I'll look into these guys and get back to you."

"I know everybody wants your time, but I wanna throw you a welcome home party. Let me know what night is good for you." Apollo leaned over and touched Johnny's shoulder. "It's good to have you home, brother."

"Thanks. It's good to be home and to see you. Do the party whenever you want. Just let me know. I think our little private crew should all have dinner real soon. I'll call you." The two men hugged goodbye. Johnny cracked his knuckles, smiled, gave a quick wink, and left.

CHAPTER TEN

The dinner party from his crew was, in every way, a truly memorable affair. It was a party that would be talked about for years. Ralphie was able to convince the owner (his brother-in-law) of Rao's, a legendary Italian restaurant on Pleasant Avenue, to close for the night. People made reservations a year in advance—but only powerful people—to get into Rao's. No one else could get in. Politicians, movie stars, and assorted members of various crime families dined there every night. There was no menu, and no one ever left without a smile on their face. The night of the welcome home party, the place was filled with friendly faces who were genuinely glad to see Johnny Angel home at last. There was a large table set up buffet-style with all of Johnny's favorite foods. It consisted of Rao's world-famous seafood salad, baked clams oreganata, branzino in a salted crust, just to name a few of the seafood classics served there—all Johnny's favorites.

Before Ralphie gave Johnny an envelope from all the guys, he handed him a burlap sack full of dimes. "Here's a little something for your coming home present," he said, "just like the old days." He handed Johnny the sack of coins.

Johnny smiled. Some things never change. "We were ten years old back then." After everyone had a good laugh, Ralph handed him the real envelope. Johnny was sure that Ralph made everyone kick in something, and he was equally positive that Ralphie did not put anything in the envelope himself. Johnny believed that Ralphie cared about him and very much liked him but he was too cheap to part with any of his cash. "Thanks, Ralphie, I truly appreciate it." He kissed Ralphie on each cheek and hugged him.

Paul, one of the many men in Ralphie's crew and in charge of the evening's festivities, spared no expense with the eight-course meal. And to top it off, he brought out a four-tier cake with a man walking out of prison on top. The guys all had a good laugh. The party was strictly for the mafia crew that Johnny belonged to—the Harlem Crew. A dozen made men that were a tight group and all friends for many years.

As the party began to quiet down, Johnny walked up to Danny and looped his arm through Danny's, walking him away from the crowd. "What's the deal with La Camorra?"

Danny smiled and said, "You spoke to Apollo, I see. After you meet with Boris tomorrow, me, you, and Nicky will sit down with them."

"I'm not sure I wanna sit down with them, Danny. What's really happening?"

"Just keep an open mind, would you? This could be a good thing."

Johnny stopped walking and turned to look at Danny. "Does Ralphie know?"

"No. I don't think we need to go on record with this, Johnny. Hear us out first before you make any conclusions."

"Us—don't you mean 'them'?"

"You know what I mean, Johnny."

"These are dangerous people, Danny."

"Yeah, and we're not?"

"Shit, Danny," Johnny said, throwing his arms in the air for emphasis, "you've been getting me in trouble all my life. No sense in trying to stop you now."

Danny put his hand to his forehead and said, "Oh, I can't believe you just said that. Nicky, Nicky, come here!"

Nicky had been talking to a few of the guys in the crew. He came walking over with a look on his face of 'don't get me in the middle of your arguing.' "What?" he asked suspiciously.

"This guy," Danny said, pointing to Johnny, "just said that I have been getting him into trouble his whole life. Can you believe that?"

Nicky shook his head. "He's wrong. You've been getting us into trouble your whole life."

"Oh, both of you, go fuck yourself." The three old friends laughed and joined everyone else again. When Johnny left the party, he was full and happy. He was also concerned about what Danny was into with the Camorra, the Naples version of the mafia. He decided to go home to Teresa and Angela. He was really enjoying Angel's company. Teresa, too for that matter—but Angel was growing fast, and he'd missed a lot of it. Like most guys in his line of work, Johnny wondered if he'd ever get old watching his family grow and start their own families.

***

Johnny was in Little Italy visiting friends. It was a beautiful day, so he decided to walk over to Houston Street when it was time to meet Boris at Katz's deli. As he approached, he noticed Boris sitting in a big black Cadillac right in front of the deli. Boris noticed Johnny and got out to hug him. Boris kissed both of Johnny's cheeks and led him inside the famous landmark restaurant.

"I'm sorry I made the meet here," he said, "but it was necessary at the time, though it's not anymore."

Johnny ordered a pastrami sandwich, a vanilla egg cream and grabbed a plate of pickles. Boris explained the whole problem to Johnny and everything that had taken place. "The heat will be on for a few days, but I am now in charge of both brotherhoods. Georgie is my man there, and everyone is fine with him being boss."

"Nice work," Johnny said, nodding his head in approval. "Are you sure this Georgie won't turn on you?" Johnny took another bite of his huge sandwich.

Boris was munching on a pickle and stopped when Johnny asked that question. "Quite sure, I brought him to America and took care of him from day one."

"Yes, I understand that, but as crazy as it sounds, many people secretly despise that. It's the old 'bring home a dying snake and nursing him back to health still won't ensure him not biting you' situation. Once George starts reeling in the power you have made available to him, it might go to his head. If you took a dog off the street that was freezing and starving and brought him home and warmed him, fed him, and gave him a home, that dog would never ever bite you. And that, my friend, is the difference between man and dog."

"Well, I guess only time will tell. We do have one problem we need to address. The Lucchese Family. I'm not quite sure how to handle that one."

Johnny laughed. "I figured you'd get to that sooner or later. What do you have in mind?" Boris paused, then bit into his pickle. Johnny knew he was thinking about how to say what he wanted to say. "Now that I'm in charge and our brotherhood is with you, I think you should get the cut of our new joint venture." "That won't work, Boris, but I do thank you for the effort. I can't knock them out of the picture. And besides, only you and George know who's in charge. You can't let them know you were behind this. They'd take you out for sure. You might have Georgie tell them that he is doing some business with you. This way, we can start cutting their take without cutting them out."

Boris was not in agreement, but he loved and respected Johnny. He would not resist too much. "To the victors go the spoils."

Johnny put his sandwich down and smiled. "Yes, and to the greedy goes the bullet." He would meet Boris in the middle on this one. He continued, "Take a cut of their action for winning and allowing them to keep earning. You had the right to kill them all so I can defend that when I sit down with them. Just keep in mind that the Lucchese's are a wild bunch who shoot first and ask questions later."

Boris nodded his head in approval. He reached into his sports coat and took out an envelope. "Here's something from me to welcome you home." Johnny took the money and said,

"Thank you, my friend. I also want to thank you for all you've done the whole time I was gone. It means a lot to me."

Boris laughed. "I sent a case of caviar to the warden's wife and signed it 'From those of us that love an Angel.'"

"I know." Johnny nodded. "I got called to the warden's office. He said that was a bribe and not very wise of me."

"Oh shit, what did you say?" "I told him that I was there to do my time, and I didn't want anything from him, nor did I expect anything. I couldn't help it if I had friends that tried to look out for me. I told him to keep the caviar because I don't know anything about it—and that if I were trying to bribe him, I'd use money, not fish eggs."

Boris roared with laughter. "Oh shit, that's funny. I do need your help, though with something else." He looked around. The place was always packed. It didn't matter if it were three in the afternoon or three in the morning—Katz's Deli was packed. He leaned in closer and whispered, "I've got a load of cash that I can't do anything with. I need to make it good money."

"How much needs to be cleaned?" Johnny asked.

"Three million," replied Boris.

Johnny shook his head. "That's gonna cost you almost half a million. I think they're getting fifteen percent now."

"Yeah, but it's worth it for clean money. Can you find out for me?"

"Sure, give me a few days to work on it. I'm afraid I gotta run. I want to have dinner with you and the others. Let's try for Thursday night." Johnny took the last bite of his pastrami sandwich, washed it down with the last of his vanilla egg cream, then jokingly asked, "You think you can stay alive 'til then?"

Boris laughed, pickle in hand. "Your made guy with the Lucchese Family is the one that needs to worry about staying alive." He was waving the pickle as he talked.

Johnny snatched the pickle from him and took a bite, and said, "Don't start no shit with them. We'll talk Thursday." He dropped the rest of the pickle onto the table and walked out.

"That works for me. Just let me know where and when!" Boris yelled back. He shook his head and laughed. It was sure good to have Johnny Angel back home. He was the only man alive that could get away with stealing his pickle.

As Johnny walked back down to Little Italy, he thought about the meeting that was about to take place. He was not sure how he felt about it, so he decided to see what they had to say. He trusted Danny and Nicky with his life and loved them dearly, but they were not the best judge of characters. Nicky was all brute and had no brains, and Danny was too greedy to look at things objectively.

***

La Camorra, "The Neapolitan Mafia," was about seven thousand members strong—but that was mostly in Naples, Italy. Here in the States, they were not as big as the American mafia and nowhere as deeply embedded in society. In fact, they were less than a hundred spread around the country. There was a small crew in Miami, Los Angeles, Houston, and Buffalo. The largest crew was the New York City crew, who were in charge of all the crews in the States. The boss was Giovanni Brusca, but everyone called him "JB." He was a short man, five feet six inches—but deadly. He had the respect of all Camorra. His underboss was Anthony "Ice Pick" Sparaceca, rumored to have killed a dozen guys using an ice pick. The meeting was in a warehouse in the Bronx.

When Danny, Nicky, and Johnny arrived, JB and Ice Pick were already there waiting. The outside of the warehouse belied how nice the set-up was on the inside. It was decked out in the latest contemporary furniture and art. Johnny was impressed. Danny introduced Johnny, and they all sat down at a long table in what looked like a conference room to Johnny.

"It is an honor to finally meet you, Johnny Angel. You are the most respected of all of our kind. What can I get you gentlemen to drink?" JB asked. Anthony got up and brought back drinks for everyone.

He sat back down, and JB began. "Johnny, I know you are a no-nonsense man. I'd like to speak openly, and I want you to know that I mean no disrespect, but I want to talk a little about facts."

"Please feel free to speak your mind, JB."

JB took a sip of his espresso. "Thank you. This thing of ours here in America is weak and cannot be trusted. Nearly twenty percent of the members are in the Federal Witness Protection Program. I think it's safe to say that another third are cooperating already or will someday."

Johnny interrupted, saying, "I thought you were gonna stick to facts?"

"Touché," JB said with a smile. "Facts and hypotheses, if you'll indulge me. We of the Camorra have not had one defector ever, and need I remind you we are in existence for at least two hundred years longer than you and yours. We date back to the mid-1500s. One reason for no rats is if we ever did have a defector, we would kill their whole family. You Americans are restricted by your rules, and that is a weakness."

"And the point of this whole historic speech is?"

This time JB laughed, and Johnny realized this man was a likable kind of guy but dangerous as a rattlesnake. His accent was slight, his English good. "The point, my friend, is that we are trying to spread our wings here in America, the land of the brave, the home of the free—and tons of money. The fruits here are plentiful, and we'd like to wet our beak too."

"So who's stopping you? What is it you want from us?"

"We'd like your loyalty."

"We are already spoken for in the loyalty department, as you well know."

"Yes, yes, and I am not asking you to do anything that would hurt your family—but quite the opposite. We can't very well form alliances with just any American Mafioso, so we choose you, Danny, and Nicky. You three will protect us from all others of our kind by shielding us. No one but you three will know us, and all of our soldiers around the country will be forbidden to do business with the American Mafia. Your network is vast and well established but more importantly is you, Mr. Johnny Angel. You are a very unique Mafioso. Your standup reputation is impeccable. Your balls and fearlessness might only be outdone by your cunning and your intelligence. "You are not just a member of La Cosa Nostra, but you are equally accepted in the Russian Bratva, The Chinese Triads, The Colombian Cartel, and the biggest Black-organized crime group in New York City. You have achieved something that no other before you has ever been able to do. It is truly amazing."

Johnny smiled, leaned back, and said, "Wow, if I'm all that, then you must be offering me a lot of money right now."

JB laughed at the comment and replied, "I am. What I really want are your United Nations crews. We can do business with you three, but I don't trust anyone else in this thing of ours. I only ask that when you speak with your capo or any other of your brothers in La Famiglia, that you never mention Camorra or me and Anthony."

"How did you guys hook up with Danny?" Johnny asked, curious.

JB gestured for Danny to explain. "You remember when we were kids, my cousin Sal came and stayed the summer from Italy?"

"Yeah, wasn't he the one that we had a highspeed car chase with the cops when we were kids?"

"Yeah, that's him. Well, he's a made guy with La Camorra, so he introduced us."

"Little Sal is straightened out?"

It was JB who answered now. "Yes, he got good training hanging with you guys for a summer. He is a capo now with his own crew."

Johnny nodded. He wondered if their main thing was drugs. It most likely is, he figured. He knew Lee would not need another supplier. "The triads will not be interested in your product."

"Our product, as you put it, is many different things—and I can assure you that all of your people will be interested in doing business with us."

As much as he'd tried, he still could not find it in him to dislike this guy. "Okay, JB, what does this alliance do for us?" "You're in for ten percent of all the money we make with your guys—forever. Once a month, we'll bring you an envelope, and all you gotta do is hook us up and keep everyone else away from us. If it ever comes up, we'll let it be known that we're with you, and that's where we intend to stay."

Johnny stood up, put his hand out, and said, "I will get back to you on Friday, same time, same channel."

JB and Anthony stood up, as did Nick and Danny. JB took Johnny's hand and said, "I'll look forward to it then."

When they got out on the street, Danny asked, "Well, what do you think?"

"What have you been doing with them so far?"

Danny smiled and said, "Just moving a little dope and coke."

"And Sal okayed them?"

"Sure. Why you don't like these guys?"

"Actually, I do like them. Let me talk with the boys. We'll see where this goes." They got in the car and left.

Johnny was anxious to see Theresa and Angel. "Drop me off in Harlem," he said and leaned back to relax. "This JB is quite the character, Danny. I'm sure he has the balls—but let's see if he has the brains to match."

CHAPTER ELEVEN

Lee was having dinner with his top lieutenants in the back part of a fancy Chinese restaurant. At the next table, five bodyguards sat watching everything. Johnny wanted to surprise Lee and test his security at the same time. Looking through the window, he quickly noticed the table with the bodyguards, so he went around back to the alleyway and walked into the kitchen. He grabbed a white chef's jacket and hat along with an empty tray that happened to be sitting right on the inside. A worker must have been on a break. He walked right past everyone in the kitchen. No one questioned him. He entered the dining room, and with his back to Lee's table, he made his way right up to Lee and said, "Bang, you're dead," with his finger next to Lee's temple. Lee looked shocked and then averted his eyes upward—and a big smile came across his face.

"Very good," Lee said as he stood up to embrace Johnny. "How did you get past my lazy men?"

"They were being lazy." Johnny quickly took off the hat and chef's jacket and laid it on the side of their table. The other three men stood to shake Johnny's hand and welcomed him home. They excused themselves and moved to the table with the bodyguards so Lee and Johnny could have some privacy.

"Anguo, make sure you always post someone in the kitchen, so this never happens again," Lee warned, pointing his finger at him. He was not happy that someone got in so easily—but at least it was just his old friend. "So, my friend, do you plan on staying with us for a while, or is the allure of prison just too much for you?"

Johnny laughed. "You're the one that can't handle prison unless I'm there to protect you. For me, it's just an occupational hazard. You know, like a carpenter bangs his finger or an electrician shocks himself. Me? I wind up in the joint."

Lee shook his head. "Johnny, they don't make guys like you anymore. You're the last of the real gangsters. That's why I always loved you."

"Don't start getting teary-eyed on me, okay?"

"Oh, don't worry. I know the great Johnny Angel can't talk about his feelings—too macho. Why you here? To see how much you can get for a welcome home gift? Of course not. You're here because you missed me and could not wait to see me. Now, if that's not feeling, what is?" Lee was laughing, watching Johnny squirm and trying not to react with his emotions.

Johnny shook his head. "I see you're still an asshole when you wanna be."

Lee pounded the table with an open hand. "I am Chinese Godfather, and you can get whacked talking like that to me!" Lee said, pointing a finger at Johnny and trying to keep a straight face. The other patrons in the restaurant overheard and were all nervously watching.

"How 'bout I take that Chinese Godfather finger of yours and shove it right up your Chinese ass!"

Lee made a face and said, "That would ruin my meal." Both men cracked up laughing. The other patrons saw there was no more show and returned to eating their meals.

"You are too stupid," Johnny replied. This bond from childhood was deep, and Lee appreciated it very much.

"I haven't gotten stupid silly like this in the last five years you've been gone. I've missed you, my friend." Johnny realized that Lee had to maintain an aura of authority being the Dragon Head of the Tongs—and being silly did not fall into that category.

"And I have missed you, Meng Chang," Johnny said, using Lee's real name that no one ever used.

"My sister asked about you last week." Lee changed his voice to sound like a woman. "When is Johnny Angel coming home?"

Johnny's face lit up thinking about Sing, Lee's sister. She was such a good kid and pretty as a flower. She always had a big crush on Johnny when they were kids. "How is my little flower?" Johnny had never tried to be with her out of respect to Lee even though Lee, over the years, had suggested they get married.

"She's not married anymore. Her poor husband had a heart attack and died."

"Oh, sorry to hear that."

"You are the only one that is sorry about that, including Sing. She will be happy to see you."

Johnny smiled. "I look forward to seeing her also. I want to have a meeting Thursday night. Me, you and the boys."

"Ah, I will look forward to it. Johnny, I know you just got back, and I hate to bother you already, but I'd like for you to sit down with the Gambino Family. I'm having some trouble with Yakuza, and before it gets out of hand, we should address it."

Johnny frowned and thought for a minute. "That's not the Gambino's; it's the Columbo's. The Yakuza is with the Columbo Family, but either way, I'll get in touch."

"Gambino, Columbo, it's all the same shit—a bunch of Wops."

"Chang Cheng-Ming Mang, all the same shit- a bunch of fucking slant-eyed Gooks." This was a rib game they played for thirty years, and they both started laughing again. They only did it when they were alone, but since they haven't seen each other for five years, it seemed okay.

The two old friends ate dinner and talked of old times, always comparing the past to the present. Lee had made the transition well. Johnny was happy to see how good he looked and how well he was doing.

"You always had a brain, Lee. I knew you would do well in life."

"And you, my friend, always had balls bigger than a bull. I knew you would do well."

"So with your brains and my balls, we should own this town by now. What went wrong?"

"Ah, but we do own this town. Nothing went wrong. Everything is as it should be."

Johnny made a face and said, "Don't start with all that Confucius stuff now-or what do you call it, Dow Jones?"

Lee was laughing hard, trying to catch his breath before he could answer, "That would be Tao Te Ching."

The night was wrapping up. Johnny got up. "Thanks for the duck soup. Don't forget Thursday night."

"I wouldn't miss it for the world. I have an envelope for you. I'll bring it then." Johnny walked past the other table and bowed slightly. Lee's men responded with the same show of respect. They knew Johnny Angel was an important man, and we're sure they would see him again.

CHAPTER TWELVE

Yankee was in charge of security for the dinner party of the five leaders. There were two main concerns whenever they all got together. The first was to make sure law enforcement did not catch wind of their meeting. No one knew where they were going to meet until they got there; not even Johnny. Yankee was sure to not even let his own men know. He chose a small Cuban restaurant on 2nd Avenue between 63rd and 64th Streets.

One hour before the dinner, he had the place swept for bugs and then posted a few men inside and out for extra security—no sense in taking chances. A driver picked up each of the other four leaders and drove around for about twenty minutes before entering an underground parking garage. The leader was switched into another vehicle and then driven to the location. Yankee had paid the restaurant owner not to open to the public that night, so the only people there at the meeting time were the five old friends and a dozen of Yankee's top guns. Three were posted in the kitchen, and one of those watched everything the chefs put in the food. This took care of the second main concern: security.

Boris was the last to arrive, and the rest of the men all got on his case for being late.

"How can you blame me? I had nothing to do about getting here? It's Yankee's fault," Boris said in his own defense.

They all enjoyed these rare gatherings. Even though the four leaders had done business together over the last five years and have even met one another a few times, they had not all gotten together like this since Johnny's farewell party the night before he went to prison. So, this special evening was being celebrated enthusiastically as they drank and joked around with one another.

Johnny stood up and said, "A toast to my friends! I'm glad to see you are all alive and well, and you have all prospered during my vacation. Salute!"

The resounding "Salute" was heartfelt, and Yankee yelled out, "Do you plan on staying home this time?" followed by cheers and chants of "Yes! Yes! Yes!" The staff started to bring out the food. They brought a large bowl of salad followed by trays of roasted pork, crab stew, breaded fried steak, and chicken in a bittersweet sauce with yellow rice and black beans. Every morsel was delicious. An hour later, they were drinking strong black espresso and letting all the food settle.

Johnny stood again and said, "Good choice Yankee. Everything was great. So, gentlemen, we need to talk about joining forces with a new group. They are new to us but not new at all. Is anyone familiar with La Camorra?"

"Is that the guys with Danny?" Apollo asked.

"Yes, but let me explain who they are. La Camorra is the Mafia from Naples, Italy. They are powerful, international, and deadly. They asked for a meeting with me. Danny's cousin, whom I have met before, is one of them, and he set it up. They were not interested in doing business with the American Mafia. He explained that they wanted to work with him so they could have access to all of you. They are serious men, and they are only interested in the serious men who sit around this table, you guys."

Lee said, "Their business is heroin, and it would conflict with mine." He raised his hands up.

"I already told them that, but they say there are so many things you guys can work on with them."

"What do you think, Johnny?" asked Yankee.

"I like them. I think we should try working with them. Let's see what they can bring to the table." He nodded his head. They all agreed that if Johnny was on board, they were on board. Apollo was the only one that was strictly local. The others were international in their dealings, and Johnny thought this could be a good deal for them.

"Okay then, I'll be coming by to see each of you with JB, who is the boss, and Anthony, who is the under-boss. We'll set things up, and after the initial meet, you'll want to stay onceremoved at the very least, so have one of your guys ready."

The night went on for a couple of more hours, and then the men left in the limousines that were waiting outside. Johnny stayed behind a little longer with Yankee once everyone had left. It had been a productive evening, and he had enjoyed every minute of it. The two friends talked for another forty minutes.

At one point, Yankee said, "I have to go back to Colombia, so bring these Camorra guys to me first, and then I will leave."

"How long will you be gone for?"

"A few weeks at the most."

"We'll come see you Saturday night around eight. Okay for you?"

"That'll work." The two men shook hands and hugged before leaving.

***

While the dinner party was going on, there was another meeting taking place at a restaurant in Queens. JB, Anthony, and four other Camorra were figuring out their next move.

"What if Johnny Angel don't deliver?" Anthony asked.

"I think he will," replied JB as he took a sip of his espresso.

"But if he doesn't?"

"Then we'll need to replace all five of those characters—but my gut tells me Johnny Angel is with us."

"The American Mafia is weak. We should replace all of them," said one of the men at the table.

"Yes," JB replied, nodding his head, "but unfortunately, we need them. This is their country and their connections. It would be most difficult, if not impossible, to replace all of that. There are still a few good old-fashioned soldiers here in America, and Johnny Angel is one of them."

"You never know until the shit hits the fan, and then it's too late."

"Yes, but this is the life we chose, so we'll play the hand that was dealt us." Then turning to Anthony as if an afterthought, he said, "Anthony, you start working on plan B. I doubt it will come to that, but we must be ready.

***

Theresa and Angela were watching a movie when Johnny came home. He sat down between them, and Angela laid her head on his lap while Theresa rested hers on his shoulder. Johnny rubbed his daughter's head and asked, "What are you guys watching?"

"Some movie about a girl who has a racehorse," replied his daughter.

"Is it good?"

Angela sat back up and looked him in the eyes, and said, "Yes, Daddy, now be quiet please and let us watch it."

"Oh, well, excuse me," he replied, putting his hands up.

Theresa laughed and said, "We're serious about our movies here."

"I can see that. I'm gonna go take a shower." Johnny excused himself to rinse off and brushed his teeth and shave, and by the time he was done, the movie was over, and the girls were waiting for him.

"She's waiting up for you to tuck her in," Theresa said with a big smile. The family life is what she always wanted, and these past five years, she had dreamed of the day Johnny would be out and home with them. It made her heart flutter just watching the two of them. She wondered how long they would be able to keep him.

Theresa knew that a man like Johnny was not the type to settle down. He was a good man, and she knew in his own way he loved them—but the streets were his life. He could be back in prison tomorrow or dead the following day. She was always careful talking with Angel about future plans concerning Johnny. Her pat answer was they'd have to talk to him about it.

After they put Angel to bed, Theresa and Johnny had a drink and talked for a while, sitting on the couch. "I thought if you didn't have any plans, maybe we can go away for a few days?"

Johnny made a face and said, "Where you wanna go?"

"I don't care, but it would be nice to have your undivided attention and take Angel to a nice tropical place. I'm sure you could use a little vacation too. Nothing long, just a few days."

"That would be nice, but I've got a lot of catching up to do first. We'll see." Johnny noticed the disappointment on her face.

"Hey," he said with a smile, "aren't you happy that I'm here?"

"Yeah, of course, I'm just saying…."

"I hear you, baby. We'll see. If I can get away, I will. Maybe you guys should go for a week, and I'll try and meet you for a few days."

"No, that's okay. We want to go with you. If you can't make it, we'll wait."

"All right, let's go to bed then." They made love, and to Theresa, it was beautiful. She lay there afterward, basking in his scent. She thought how nice it would be to spend some time on a beach with him and Angel. She smiled, picturing them playing in the soft waves as a nice salty breeze kept them cool. Her last thought as she fell asleep was rubbing lotion on Johnny's back.

***

Michael "Little Mike" DeStaffino was a soldier in the Lucchese Family. He was Vip's connection to the mafia and earned with the Solntsevskaya Bratva. Johnny Angel had the other Russian crew, and Little Mike wanted to make sure the killing of Vip and his men was not a move by them to take over now that Johnny was out of the joint. When he found out that Vladimir and all his men were dead, he quickly called a meeting with Georgie Z, figuring that Georgie was the next in command. Of course, he had no idea that Georgie was really Boris's guy.

As he parked his car, he tried to figure out what happened. These fucking Russians were crazy, and any scenario was possible with them. One thing he was sure of was that they belonged to him, and that was not going to change. He had met Georgie before but really did not know him well. He decided to give Georgie the benefit of the doubt until he figured out what kind of guy he was. When he entered the restaurant, he saw Georgie was there waiting for him. He expected nothing less. The two men shook hands, and Little Mike got right down to business.

"I don't wanna know what happened and who did what to who. Your in-house disputes should always be run by me first before any moves are made. My only concern is that you understand that this crew is with me."

"I'm fully aware of that, Mike. My problem is that since Boris won this war, we've had to make concessions to save whatever is left of our Brotherhood."

"What concessions?" Mike asked, starting to lose his patience.

"Twenty-five percent of our take goes to Boris. I think you need to know that Boris did not start this. It was Vladimir who tried to take Boris out, but somehow, the tables turned, and they nearly wiped us out."

Little Mike was mad, spitting as he talked. "You don't give those sons of a bitches nothing. You hear me! I'll call you in a few days, but I'll straighten this out. From now on, that twenty-five percent comes to us since you're so eager to give up money." Mike stood up and left without a goodbye or anything. When he got in his car, he figured he had Georgie all summed up. He was definitely Boris's guy, and Johnny Angel must have been behind this whole thing. They had another thing coming if they thought he was going to sit by and let that happen.

Obviously, Johnny had been planning this the whole time he was locked up. He couldn't wait to get out and start trouble. If that's what he wanted, that's what he'd get. Little Mike pulled out of the parking space with a smile on his face. He was sure he'd have the last laugh.

CHAPTER THIRTEEN

It was hard to keep hold of the Washington Heights neighborhood. Yankee had been battling for years with the Puerto Ricans and Dominicans. Even though this neighborhood was his headquarters, it was nothing like Apollo had in Harlem. Yankee did not control the street-level drug dealing here. In fact, Yankee did not control street-level dealing anywhere. He was an importer, and a long time ago, at Johnny's strong suggestion, he had relinquished all street selling, giving his men the orders not to sell at that level.

The Dominicans ran most of Washington Heights. The Puerto Ricans got whatever was leftover. Throughout the years, Yankee was able to form an alliance with these groups. The fact that he represented the most powerful Colombian Cartel was a good reason for making a business agreement that worked well for everyone. The Dominicans were ruthless in their pursuit of power. Yankee posed no threat to any of the gangs in the area. He was able to instead negotiate good deals with the Dominicans, so everyone was happy.

No one really wanted to deal with the Dominicans, but somehow Yankee managed it and managed it well. Over the years, the different factions came to rely on Yankee to mediate problems and quarrels. He became the elder statesman of Washington Heights. Though he did not seek the job, it was a good way to keep a hold of his kingdom.

Raul Romero was the current Dominican boss, and in Yankee's opinion, he was the deadliest. He was young and wild, but for some reason, he looked up to Yankee like an uncle or mentor, and over the past year, Yankee had actually started to like him. Raul walked into the Polo Grounds Bar and left a half dozen of his men to wait outside. He walked to the back table and said, "Tell Yankee I'm here."

He was frisked and then ushered into the office where Yankee was talking on the phone. He motioned for Raul to have a seat, and as soon as he hung up the phone, he got up and said, "Hello, my friend, how are you?"

"Good Yankee, but I have a problem—or more like you have a problem. One of your guys is moving some weight on the side. Did you know that?"

"Of course, I didn't. You already know that, so why do you ask?" Raul smiled. He knew Yankee was unaware of what one of his men was doing. He just needed to make sure.

He cocked his head to the side and said, "My apologies, it's just an old habit of not trusting people. I knew you didn't know. I should've just told you instead of asking you that stupid question."

Yankee waved his hand in a gesture that said to forget about it. "Who is it?" he asked.

"Eddie Torres. If it helps you any, it is not your dope. It's from a Cuban in Miami. I have not been able to find out who is supplying him; not sure exactly yet."

Yankee nodded his head and said, "Thanks, Raul, I'll take it from here. I appreciate you coming in and telling me."

"Sorry to bring you bad news, but in this business, it seems to happen more often than not. These guys see all this cash, easy money, what the fuck. They don't think about the long term. People get killed doing shit like that, right Yankee?"

Yankee looked up from behind his desk and gave Raul a blank empty stare that said absolutely nothing.

"By the way, I need another load this week."

"You want ten or twenty?" "How much do I save if I get twenty?" "You'll save thirty G's if you take twenty."

Raul made a face and said, "Tempting, but it's too much to sit on. Just give me ten."

"You got it." They made small talk for a few more minutes, and Raul left. Yankee sat quietly, thinking about the news Raul brought. What Cuban in Miami was Eddie doing business with? There were many Cubans moving coke in Miami, and one of the biggest crews was run by Luis Santiago. Santiago had worked with Yankee for many years, and Yankee was sure Luis would not sell to one of his men. Yankee considered Santiago a loyal friend and ally and knew he would help if Yankee needed him. He picked up his cell phone and called his main man Tito.

"Find George and Juan. We need to talk." Yankee figured it would take them an hour to get there, so he went to his girlfriend's house for a quickie. When he returned to the bar, his three lieutenants were there waiting for him. Yankee sat behind his desk and lit a big fat Cuban cigar. "Juan, Eddie Torres is one of your guys, right?"

Juan had the feeling he was about to get some bad news. "Yes," was all he said. He waited to hear what this was all about.

"He's moving shit here in Manhattan, getting supplied by a Cuban in Miami."

Yankee watched Juan's face to make sure he was truly surprised. Yankee trusted Juan, but he knew that you never know in this life when someone is plotting behind your back. Juan shook his head. "That stupid fuck! What should I do?"

"Bring him here. We will question him. Who knows, maybe my sources are lying. Maybe Eddie fucked the guy's wife. Who knows? Let's see what he has to say for himself. After all, we're not animals, but if he lies, then he'll have to go. When we are done with him, we will leave him in the gutter. That's where a traitor like that belongs. Let's make him be an example for the others.

***

Joseph "Joe Dogs" Dogalatte sipped his espresso and looked over at Johnny. "So you're saying the Triads are ready to go to war?"

Johnny smiled. Joe was a likable guy, but he had a way about him that always rubbed Johnny the wrong way. The two soldiers had known each other for years back when there was a private casino that all five families had a piece of. The casino was set up in East Harlem, so Johnny was in charge of security. Joe Dogs was the Columbo Family's man at the casino, so they worked together for a couple of years. Even back then, Joe would always answer a question with a question. When they first met, Johnny had thought Joe was being a smart ass and immediately did not like him, but he soon realized that was just the way he was.

They never became great friends, but they did generally like each other. Like co-workers anywhere, they got along did the job. "What are you smiling about?" asked Joe.

"Nothing, I was just thinking that we're getting old. Look, these Yakuza guys are with you, right?"

Johnny replied and smiled. "They ain't with nobody, Johnny. They associate with us, and we earn a little from some of their things, but it ain't like the old days when we ran everything. Maybe you been away too long."

"So, are you going to bat for these guys or not, Joey?"

"I can't speak for them, Johnny. I can only bring back what you offer and get back with you after that."

Johnny figured he would press the situation since Joe Dogs was tip-toeing around this mess. "We're not offering nothing but to allow them to live, Joe. My guys are not gonna give up a piece of their action to a handful of Yakuza. We've got over a thousand men. We could crush them. They just need to stay away from places that are already established by my guys. Tell them to open their own gambling joint if that's what they want to do."

"Come on, Johnny Angel, give me something to work with here. You know better than me they're not gonna be okay with this. In the same respect, you're taking money away from us. These guys are on record with us."

"I just asked you if they're with you, and you said no, now you say yeah. If they're on record with you, then they're with you. That makes it a little different story. They can have the Queens joint for themselves if they agree to not bother any more established places—and if they break their word, there won't be any more talking."

"What about the Brooklyn joint? They bring a lot of business there." "They can have the Queens joint all for themselves or fifty percent of the Queens and Brooklyn joint, but they can't have both." "We'll take door number two, fifty percent of both joints, done deal." Joe stuck out his hand, and Johnny shook it. Johnny thought that Joe was a funny guy. One minute he could not speak for the Yakuza, and the next, he was shaking on a deal for them. There was no sense in pressing the situation. It was just the way Joe Dogs did things. Go figure. But truth be told, Joe Dogs dancing around left a bad taste in Johnny Angel's mouth. One of the many reasons for Johnny's success in this business was a long and very accurate memory.

"I heard you were away with Mookie. How's he doing?" Mookie was a made guy from Joe's Family and the same crew.

Johnny laughed and said, "He's as crazy as ever. Somehow, he bribed this hack to pull us upfront to the offices one night after everyone was gone and we had cheeseburgers delivered by three hookers. Me, Mookie, Angie the Pipe, and Davey Green Eyes are eating burgers and getting a blow job. Everyone there loves Mookie. Send my love, would you?"

"Sure thing. He gets out next year, I think. Who's Davey Green Eyes? Is he a friend of ours?"

"Yeah, with the Gambino's. He's another fucking nut job. We had some good times up there. Well, it was good to see you, my friend. I gotta go."

"Yeah, Johnny, always a pleasure. Thanks."

Johnny went back up to Harlem to the clubhouse. He and Ralphie took a walk as Johnny explained the deal he cut with Joe Dogs. When they arrived at a local café, they sat down in a booth so Ralph could rest a minute. He was out of breath and looked pale and out of the blue. "Are you okay?" Johnny asked with true concern.

Ralph shook his head and said, "No, I can hardly breathe." He grabbed his chest, let out a moan, and collapsed to the ground with a massive heart attack. The man that had mentored Johnny since he was a kid and the only man that Johnny would have truly died for now lay dead on the sidewalk. Johnny bent down and closed the eyes of his captain Ralphie Arms. He made the sign of the cross and said a silent prayer.

CHAPTER FOURTEEN

Jessie "Jessie James" Bradley was the number two man in Apollo's organization. The crew of sixty that worked for Apollo answered directly to Jessie, and only Jessie went to Apollo. The two men had been friends for forty years, and people had always referred to Jessie as Apollo's bulldog. Years ago, when Apollo first started structuring his organization, Jessie was opposed to it. He was way too much gangster for this kind of corporate structure, but he eventually came to realize that this was a good thing. Ever since they were kids, he always knew that Apollo had the brains. Together they had created a good life, so he was disappointed that he had to bring the bad news to Apollo now as he entered the office. Apollo stood up and smiled as his oldest friend walked in. They shook hands, and Apollo immediately sensed something was off.

He asked, "What's wrong?"

"Two crackheads killed some guy last night on 128th and Amsterdam." When Apollo did not say anything, he continued, "Tried to rob him and the guy put up a fight. They stabbed him about thirty times."

Apollo's face coiled in anger. "Find them before the cops do. We need to make examples of these assholes."

"I'm already on it. I think Marvin knows one of the crackheads."

"What makes you say that?" Apollo asked.

"I think it's his wife's brother," Jesse answered, not really wanting to until he knew for sure, but he would not lie to Apollo. "She told Marvin that her brother Deon stabbed someone last night."

"Ah, shit!" Apollo did not like the idea of killing one of his men's family members.

"Tell Marvin to get this kid and beat his ass, then take him upstate to the mountains and keep him up there for a couple of months. When he's clean, he can come back—and this is the only pass he'll get. He stays away until he's sober a while. Of course, he has to give up the other guy so we can take care of business there."

Jessie nodded. "Where upstate should he bring him?"

"I'll get the address and directions. My friend has a farm upstate. This kid will work for free shoveling shit, cleaning out the stables, and he can't leave the farm. Marvin will check on him every weekend. That's it. He takes it or leaves it."

"And if he leaves it?" Jesse asked, already knowing the answer. Apollo made a face.

"It's our deal, or he pays the devil."

Jessie shook his head. "Looks like it's gonna be one of those weekends." He quickly left to get Marvin and take care of this problem.

***

This time, the meeting was in an apartment on Webster Avenue in the Bronx. Johnny made note of the fact that these guys did not meet and conduct business in the open as his American Mafia guys did. His counterparts from La Camorra did things the old-fashioned way: secretive and low-key. He liked the fact that these guys were not about the ego and showing off; they respected the secret society they belonged to. There was no elevator in the old brownstone building, and Nicky complained all the way up to the sixth-floor apartment. Danny and Johnny laughed and teased him the whole way. They had been dealing with Nicky being slow all their lives; there was nothing new about that. They knocked on the apartment door and were greeted by JB and Anthony.

There was a big bowl of macaroni on the table, and JB served a plate to Johnny and then the two other men. He poured a glass of wine for everyone and sat down at the large dining room table to his own plate. Anthony had not waited for them and was already half-finished. JB lifted his wine glass and said, "I believe we have something to celebrate. Salute."

Johnny smiled as he touched the other men's glasses. "You seem quite sure of yourself."

It was JB's turn to smile. "Partnering with us is the smartest move you can make, Johnny, and I already know you're a smart man. And besides that, you cannot deny that there's a connection between us. I felt it as soon as I met you. So I am right, aren't I?"

Johnny nodded his head. "Yes, we'll give this a try and see how it works out. There are a few conditions, though."

"Of course, there are always conditions. I figured as much. What are they?" Johnny took a sip of his wine before he began. "First off, no more six-story buildings without elevators. Nicky can't handle it." They all laughed, except Nicky.

"After the initial meet, my guys won't be involved in any of the dealings. Your guys will deal with their men. The only other thing is I want you to understand that even though these people aren't friends of ours, they are friends of mine. Long-time, dear friends, and they have my support one hundred percent."

JB made a face and said, "I'm hurt that you felt the need to even say so much. I already know who they are, and your relationship with them, but my intentions are as good as I am sure yours are."

Johnny swirled a fork full of spaghetti and put it in his mouth, chewing well before he swallowed. Once again, he smiled, and not finding it necessary to apologize. He moved on. "We can meet up with everyone this weekend if you want. Monday is Ralphie's funeral, so I'll be tied up."

"Yes, I heard about that. My deepest condolences," he replied, looking at each man in turn. "It is more of a shame when one of the true soldiers dies. He was old-time Mafioso, no?"

"He was," Johnny answered with a smile, remembering his mentor. "The last of a dying breed."

"An American dying breed, not so with La Camorra. We are very much the old school way."

"I appreciate that. So how do you wanna do this?"

"Why don't we leave that up to you. Your town means it's your call."

"Fair enough." He nodded in agreement. "Call me tomorrow with an address, and we'll meet. This pasta is very good. Who made it?" Anthony beamed and spoke for the first time.

"I made it. You like?"

"It's excellent. Is that anchovies I'm tasting?" he asked as he swallowed another bite.

"Yes, but I turn them into a paste when I heat the olive oil and garlic, then tomatoes and heavy on the black pepper. I fry the whole thing. In twenty minutes, it's done."

"Bravo," Nicky said with food stuck in his teeth.

"I love it." Johnny smiled. "Salute," he said as he raised his wine glass. "Anyone who can cook this good is all right in my book." After dinner, they had espresso and a shot of Sambuca. "I apologize for having to eat and run," Johnny said, "but we need to go by and see Ralphie's wife before it gets too late."

"Ah, no problem. We will see you tomorrow then. Ciao.

***

Ivan Borsky was a despicable man. He did not have any real friends, but he had plenty of acquaintances. Boris could hardly stand him, but he was a great earner for the Brotherhood, so he was tolerated-but barely. No one liked him. Ivan was in the human trade business, trafficking women in prostitution. His organization was worldwide, and now that Mika was dead, he wanted to take over the operation in Spain before The Solntsevskaya Bratva regrouped and picked up the slack.

Southern Spain had a dozen high-dollar whore houses that Mika had supplied with women, and Ivan wanted control. He came to see Boris to try his best at working out a deal. Boris was trying to think of a way to cut out the Lucchese Family without it directly coming back on him. Ivan's idea was the perfect solution.

"How do we stand in Spain now?"

"We are strong in Barcelona, Madrid, and Seville, but Mika was strong in Granada and Malaga, which both have dozens of houses there. I can take those over, and we'll have Spain locked up."

"Go for it. Do you need any extra men?"

"No, I'm good. There might be some resistance, but I can deal with it. Or do I need to keep the peace?"

"Use our Bratva in Madrid; they are good soldiers. You handle this however you see fit. You have my full backing."

Ivan smiled. He felt a comradeship with the boss, and that made him feel special. "Thank you. I will not let the Brotherhood down."

Boris could not wait to dismiss Ivan, but he wanted to make sure of a few things. "I trust that whatever opposition you run into, you will deal with swiftly. We do not want a long, drawn-out war there; it is not good for business. I think it might also be wise to load the houses with women from Brazil and South America instead of Ukrainian women. It might confuse the ones who would oppose you."

"As you wish. Thank you again for your confidence."

"Have a good trip, Ivan—and bring back lots of money." Both men laughed, and as soon as Ivan left, Boris turned to Maxim and said, "He is a good soldier but a creepy guy. Isn't he, or is it just me?"

"He moves a lot of coke and weed brings in tons of cash. I would think we can look past his shortcomings."

"Fuck you too," Boris said, and both men enjoyed a good laugh.

CHAPTER FIFTEEN

Eddie Torres was hurting. The pain was unbearable. He was not sure how much more he could endure. They were in a basement in some building, and he was chained to the pipes hanging a foot or so off the ground. Tito, George, Juan, and Yankee were there with two other men who were working him over. After half an hour of torture, he finally broke and admitted everything.

He was doing business with a guy named Blanco, who worked for Cuban Luis in Miami. Luis was a good long-time customer of Yankee's, and Yankee was sure Luis had no idea that these two were doing deals behind his back. Looking at his men, he said, "We're through with this piece of shit. Chop his hands off and dump his ass somewhere." Yankee took out his cell phone and called a Miami number. When Luis answered, Yankee said, "Find a payphone and call me at this number."

Ten minutes later, the cell phone rang, and Luis was asking, "Something wrong?"

"Of course, there's something wrong. You got a guy named Blanco working for you?"

"Sure do. What about him?"

"He's moving shit behind your back, and it ain't ours."

"Puto! Well, he won't be doing that shit no more."

"I should hope not unless you're getting soft down there with all the sun beating on your bald head."

"It's the life we lead. What can I say?"

"Say goodbye and leave it at that, my friend."

"Adios, amigo. Gracias." Yankee was sure that this Blanco would soon be facing the same pain that Eddie Torres just did. He had an hour before the meeting with Johnny and the Camorra guys. He had enough time to stop by that little Peruvian's apartment and get a blow job. He exited the building where his bodyguards were waiting for him and got into his new Cadillac. The beaten and tortured body of Eddie Torres was not even in his thoughts any longer. He had broken the rules, and he paid the price…that was all there was to it. Pretty simple, really.

JB had called Johnny with the address, and an hour later, Yankee and Johnny were walking into a first-floor apartment in Jamaica, Queens. Anthony answered the door, and they found JB sitting on the sofa. There was a platter of Italian pastries on the table and a pot of espresso coffee. Johnny introduced Yankee, and everyone shook hands. "I'm happy to meet you, Yankee," JB said. "We have many things we can help each other with." Johnny had told Yankee that JB was a likable enough kind of guy, and he had to agree.

One look at Anthony, though, and you knew that he was a deadly man. He had the eyes of a stone-cold killer-devoid of emotion. JB fooled you with his smile and charm, making him much more dangerous than his second in command.

"I'm all ears," replied Yankee.

"Europe is wide open and a huge market for cocaine. We want the exclusive rights to the European market."

Yankee made a hand gesture and said, "We already have business there."

"Yes, and so do five other cartels. We have all the best smuggling routes there and have had them for hundreds of years now. We will close down all the other traffickers. They will not be able to use Italy as a point of entry. Granted, they will find other routes, but we can corner seventy to eighty percent of the entire European market before they do."

"So are you saying that you want to buy from us exclusively and distribute in Europe?" Yankee asked as he reached for a pastry.

"Yes, but not only buy your product—we want to distribute for your Cartel. We will safely get the product there where your people will buy it from us, and we will turn around and pay you. We also can supply you with weapons, counterfeit money, and credit cards."

"What about the U.S.?"

"You undoubtedly already have in place a good system. We are not equipped to deliver for you here in America."

"And you would take delivery in Cali, Colombia?"

"Absolutely," replied JB.

"By taking out the Italian routes, how much would this increase our distribution to Europe?"

JB smiled. "I'd say thirty percent, maybe more. Let me explain. By the time the other cartels regrouped and set new routes, we'd have the market covered. With the right prices and products, why would the buyers go back to where they were?"

Yankee nodded his head, thinking about it all. "I will go home and bring your proposition up. The final decision is not mine. You do understand that?"

"Yes, I can't ask for more than that. Thank you." Johnny had been silent the whole time, and know that this discussion seemed over, he spoke up.

"I can sure use some of that fake money."

"We are working on that right now. It's being done in Argentina. We have a General with diplomatic immunity who will bring it in for us," JB said with a smile.

Johnny noted that was the first time JB had volunteered any information. He wondered why. He knew JB was too sharp to let that slip by mistake, so he asked, "And what does that have to do with me?"

JB laughed and then took a sip of his espresso. "I see you don't miss a trick, do you, my friend? The General is on a crusade to unite families that were separated during World War II. It is a passion of his because he discovered a few years ago that he had a brother living in the States. Many Italians in those days fled to Argentina and America. He needs help, so we promised him all the help he needed in America. That's where you come in, Johnny Angel."

"Geez, thanks, JB. Anything else you signed me up for that I should know about?"

They all laughed, and JB said, "I know you are a lot like me, my friend. At least you understand that not every last thing we do is about crime. We do some charitable work as well as long as it does not interfere with our profits."

Yankee was laughing when he said, "The last charitable thing this Angel did was broke only one arm of a guy that owed him money. He wanted to break both arms, but he told the guy he was giving him a break so he could still go to work." Everyone had a good laugh over that. Johnny was shaking his head and replied, "That was twenty years ago, Yankee."

"Yes, but it's a true story, nonetheless."

**

The offices of Vigorous Enterprises Inc. were located on Canal Street and took up the whole west side of the twentieth floor. Lee sat at his desk and looked at his three top enforcers. They had been together a long time, and he valued their loyalty. Cheng, his Operations Officer, was not happy with the deal that Johnny had arranged for them.

"I'm just saying I'm not sure Johnny did the best he could for us." He looked frustrated and hesitant to speak openly, knowing the relationship Lee had with Johnny Angel.

"Do you think that Johnny sold us short?"

He did not believe that, so he said, "I do not, but I think maybe he was too quick to make peace."

"Can one ever be too quick to make peace?" asked Anguo, the Deputy Mountain Master.

Lee smiled. "Yes, one can be too quick to do anything. Quick is more of a reaction rather than a response. I do not, however, believe that Johnny acted too quickly. I know whatever he does is well thought out. Perhaps we need to look at this situation from a different point of view."

"Such as?" asked Cheng.

Lee opened his palms and raised a shoulder. He stood up to emphasize his point. "Such as is it necessary to kill all the Yakuza? Are we actually losing money because we have made them a partner in two spots? The answer to both of those questions is no. Why kill when you do not have to? I think we will soon see the business go up as a result of our new partners."

"I agree," said Cai, the Liaison Officer. "We will have the biggest, strongest game in Brooklyn and Queens, which will bring more customers…which in turn will bring more money."

Cheng was not yet convinced. "What about a sign of weakness?"

Lee shook his head. "Cheng, I did not have to be present to know one hundred percent that Johnny Angel did not negotiate out of weakness. In fact, he assured me that he let it be known that we were ready to go to war with the Yakuza if they made any more advances on our places. We would outnumber them a hundred to one if it came to war. With those odds, there can be no weakness, only strength in being willing to talk."

Cheng conceded. "Okay, I will respect the decision."

"Good," Lee said with a smile. "Now, can we talk about business? Has our shipment arrived yet?"

Anguo opened his book and replied, "We have a ship docking in Los Angeles tomorrow that is loaded with movies, music CDs, clothing, and handbags-all bootleg, of course-but the finest quality. Since the government is so occupied with the Mexican border, we also have dozens of women coming across the Canadian side to work in our houses."

They discussed the heroin coming out of the Golden Triangle and how it would enter the United States. Lee looked at his watch and said, "I have a meeting I must attend. We will talk again on Monday." Lee excused himself and headed down to the parking garage under the building. Johnny was waiting in the back seat of a Lincoln town car with blacked-out windows. The driver was Gino Tucci, Danny's younger brother. They drove to Westchester County to a house in Mt. Vernon.

JB had not used the same meeting place twice. Johnny smiled with approval as he noted the caution behind JB's every move. When they arrived, Gino pulled the car all the way up the driveway and behind the house, as instructed, so Johnny and Lee could enter the house through the back door. Anthony greeted them and led the way to the living room. After the introductions, JB offered them something to drink, and the men got down to business.

"Lee, we probably have some conflict when it comes to the heroin trade, but we can be of great value to each other. You have the market cornered on bootleg merchandise, which is a billion-dollar business. I want some of that action. When it comes to Europe, no one can produce better routes for merchandise, women, even your heroin. We can deliver all of Europe to you. We have the drug and counterfeit market locked up."

Johnny sat back on the extra soft couch and listened to JB's sales pitch. He heard it all earlier when they met with Yankee. He let the two men work out some details, and when they finished, both men seemed happy.

"Do you want to meet Apollo or Boris next?" Johnny asked.

"I don't think I can do anything with Apollo," replied JB. "He gets his coke from Yankee and heroin from Lee. I don't think it's a good idea to move the bad money or credit cards here. It'll bring too much heat."

"Okay, Boris, at five tomorrow. Does that work for you?"

"Yes, perfect, I'll call you." Everyone shook hands and went on their way, just another day at the office.

CHAPTER SIXTEEN

After everyone left the funeral home, Johnny and the whole crew gathered alone with the corpse of Ralphie Arms. It was an ancient tradition; the crew gathered to make sure the body was untouched, and everything was the way it should be. They said their final farewells and closed the coffin. Johnny looked around at the seventeen crew members. Most of them he'd known all his life. "I'm it," he said, and everyone came and kissed him on the cheek. Nicky and Danny were delighted that their lifelong friend was the new captain of the crew.

"When did you find out?" Nicky asked.

"Just this morning." Then, addressing everyone, he said, "We'll continue to meet on Tuesdays at ten in the morning—for now anyway." They all nodded their consent and left the funeral home. The F.B.I. was outside in their unmarked vans, fooling nobody, taking pictures. No one cared. Most of the guys would not continue on to the cemetery, but Johnny, Nick, and Danny did, along with three other soldiers. It was a record-breaking day of heat for June, and the sun was at its peak when the funeral procession entered the cemetery. There were sixteen flower cars lined up behind the hearse, a tribute to the memory of Ralph "Ralphie Arms" Lamontino.

As the coffin was lowered to the ground, Johnny had thoughts of the future. Were things moving too fast? He had only been out for two weeks, and so much was happening. He wondered if becoming skipper of the Harlem crew and forging an alliance with La Camorra was a conflict of interest. When he was called this morning to go see the boss, he was not sure if he was going to be whacked or not. It never crossed his mind that they would promote him to Captain. He remembered one of the many things he learned from Ralphie over the years. They were talking about a decision one of the crew members had made, and the guy said, "I keep second-guessing myself about this." Ralphie had replied that it was not bad to second guess yourself. In fact, it could be helpful and insightful. It was only bad when you started mind-fucking yourself. Johnny smiled at the thought. Ralphie always had a way with words. He would be missed for sure.

***

Jesse James had Marvin point out his brother-in-law Deon. Three guys grabbed him and threw him in the back seat of the new Caddy they were driving. They brought him to a building in the neighborhood and down to the basement. The three men and the car driver went to work on Deon. They punched and kicked him for twenty minutes but never said a word or asked any questions. When he thought he would die, Marvin finally showed up. Jesse had told Marvin that his brother-in-law was going to get a beating but that they would not kill him. He had Marvin wait a while before allowing him to enter.

"Deon, you fucked up—but I can help you," Marvin spoke softly. "Who was with you last night?"

Deon could not wait to cooperate. Anything to stop the punishing pain. "Larry Hamilton. I can tell you where to find him." As an after-thought, he added, "And point him out for you. Please, Marvin, get me out of this." He had a fat bloody lip, his left eye was swollen shut, and he had peed himself. His plea for mercy was evident in his voice.

At the same time, Deon was getting his beating, two homicide detectives were at Apollo's office asking to see him. They were led into the office, and as Apollo shook their hands, he asked,

"Can I get you something to drink?"

"No, thank you," said Detective Shackford. There was no need for introductions as all three men knew each other well. The other officer, Martin Jackie, actually once arrested Apollo years ago when he was on the drug squad. The charge did not stick, and Apollo walked.

It was Officer Jackie who spoke up. "You're looking good, Apollo."

"Thanks, gentlemen. Always a pleasure to see some of New York's finest. Tell me, for what reason do I owe this lovely visit?"

"I'm sure you're aware of the man who was killed last night," Detective Jackie said, not as a question but a fact, knowing that Apollo already knew everything that happened in Harlem.

"I did hear something about that. What's that got to do with me?" Apollo asked in as serious a voice as possible. He sat behind his desk and cracked open a can of Pepsi. Gesturing toward the detectives, he asked again, "Are you sure you don't want something to drink?"

It was Shackford who replied this time. "Look, Apollo, we know how you do things, and since this happened on your turf, we know what's up with that. The problem is we're under a lot of pressure on this one to bring the killer in. As much as we wouldn't mind a scumbag like that floating in the river, we need this one alive."

"We need your help on this one, Apollo. In your line of work, someday you might need our help— you never know," added Detective Jackie.

Apollo thought for a moment, scratched the back of his ear, and picked up his cell phone. Jessie answered, and Apollo said, "Did you pick up the first package and deliver it? Okay, good. What about the second package?

Okay, change of plans. Make sure the second package is not damaged, and then bring it here. Alive, yes, and hurry up." When he hung up, he looked at the two detectives. It was a smart move to help them because this way, he would not have to kill anyone. But there was a downside too. "There's one problem with this whole deal. One of the kids involved is related to one of my men. He's already taken a good beating and has been banished from the city. I can't give him up to you, but I can give you the one who did all the stabbing. Another hour from now, and you would have been too late."

Both detectives understood that Apollo sent men out to grab these guys. They were amazed at how fast he moved on this thing. Detective Jackie spoke up. "We need both kids, Apollo. It won't work with just one."

Apollo nodded his head. "I understand that Martin, but you'll have to get that info from the kid we're giving you. I'm not gonna give him up. You'll get the one that did the stabbing."

"Fair enough," Detective Jackie agreed. Both officers were more than glad to bring the killer in within twenty-four hours of the crime. They might even get a commendation for this. When the officers left, Apollo called Jessie and told him to bring Marvin over. He wanted to let him know that his brother-in-law was most likely going to get locked up over this, but he had a chance to take off now, or he could just lay low up at the farm.

His cell phone broke his train of thought. It was Tamika, his latest girlfriend. "Yes," he said, not really wanting to be bothered right now.

"It's Saturday night, in case you didn't notice."

"Did you call me up to tell me what day it is?"

"I wanna know if we're going out tonight, that's all." They had been together for about eighteen months now, and Apollo was quickly falling into the land of disenchantment.

"Me and a few of the guys are going to the Yankees game. I'll see how I feel when I get back."

"Well, isn't that exciting for me! Maybe I can do something really fabulous like wash your fucking clothes when you get home." Her sarcasm was very annoying. Sometimes he just wanted to punch her in the face. Lucky for her, he did not hit women.

"Fortunately for you, my house is not where you live, or I think I would have you do my laundry tonight. I'm busy now. I'll call you later." Apollo hung up before she could get another word in. He would not call Tamika anymore. It was time for someone new.

***

Johnny had just enough time after the funeral to pick up Boris and drive over to the Flatbush section of Brooklyn. Once again, J.B. had a different spot picked out for the meeting. The meeting was in a house in Bensonhurst, Brooklyn, on Bath Ave. The neighborhood was still a strong Italian area. When they were all seated, J.B. gave his speech to Boris. "I think that we can be great assets to each other. From you, Boris, we are most interested in weapons and women. On our end, we can supply you with counterfeit credit cards and money, not to mention drugs. We have that market sewn up."

Boris was all smiles as he answered, "We have all the weapons you could ever dream of, including tanks. In Europe, we can do anything when it comes to weapons; except nuclear. That might be out of our reach, at least for now."

"Oh, Boris, you disappoint me," J.B. said, and everyone laughed. "How many women can you supply?" "How many do you need? Fifty a month?"

"That would be plenty."

"Ah, no problem. We can have them in any city you'd like." The meeting went just as casual as if they were trading commodities, which of course, they were. These were not the kinds of commodities bought and sold in public markets but goods that answered the needs of ordinary people all over the world. Johnny understood the universal law of supply and demand. J.B. poured a glass of wine for himself and lifted the bottle to Johnny and Boris. "Can I offer you some wine?" he asked. Both men politely refused, and J.B. continued, "Are you familiar with Estonia?" he asked. Johnny had never heard of it, but Boris knew the country well.

"Tallinn is a good city with lots of action. We have been trying to break into the market there." Responded Boris.

J.B. laughed. "Ah, too late my friend. It is already controlled by La Camorra, except the east coast, which, as you know, is close to Russia. The Solntsevskaya Bratva have control there. Lately, they have been trying to move into our territory. Can your Brotherhood be of help there? What do you think about that?"

Boris made a face and shook his head. "I don't think we can help you there. The Solntsevskaya is the most powerful in the world, and the Baltic States is a stronghold of theirs. I am surprised that you have done so well in Estonia. That in itself is amazing."

"Yes, thank you. Well, if you think of anything, let us know. Maybe together we can take the rest of Estonia. In the meantime, let's make some money." They talked for another twenty minutes and left.

Johnny dropped Boris off and went home to Theresa and Angel. He planned on staying in tonight with them and relaxing. He would deal with all the issues of the street tomorrow—but tonight was family time. He enjoyed spending time with his daughter, and he looked forward to the evening though he had no idea what the kid had planned. Johnny smiled. He really loved his daughter.

CHAPTER SEVENTEEN

Little Mike DeStafino was so enraged by the Russians and Johnny Angel that he could taste their blood. He went to his captain to get permission to whack Johnny, but he would not give him his approval. Johnny had just been made captain of the Harlem crew, and the Lucchese family did not want to start a war with the Genovese Family—like killing one of their soldiers would certainly do. They did, however, grant Little Mike the go-ahead to hit Georgie Z. If the Genovese people did not like that, they would be powerless to do anything about it because that Russian crew belonged to the Lucchese family. His mind raced with thoughts of hitting Johnny too and making it look like it was someone else. He would keep working on that, but at least he could have his day with this Georgie piece of shit. Did he really think he could fool Little Mike DeStafino? Georgie would pay for that mistake. Mike took out his cell phone and made a call. "Meet me at the usual spot," he said and immediately hung up.

Forty minutes later, Mike walked into a café in midtown Manhattan. Paul "Russian Paul" Trenorski was there waiting for him. Even though Paul was taking orders from Georgie Z, his loyalty was still with Vladimir. The coup that took Vladimir and his top men out still left Paul with a bad taste. He was more than glad to have a sit-down with Little Mike. Neither man liked the wholesale takeover maneuver of Boris, and both men privately wondered what they could do about it. Russian Paul was happy to have a possible opening.

Mike wasted no time with small talk. "We're taking back the Brotherhood," he said, "and you will be the boss. Are you in or not?"

Paul smiled, nodded his head, and simply answered, "Yes." He knew Little Mike would make a move, and he wanted to be in on it. What he did not know was that if he had refused, Mike had two men waiting outside for him. If Paul Trenorski walked out of the café without Mike beside him, he would not have made it to his car.

"You got a couple of guys we can use on this?" Mike asked.

"I do."

"Are they stand-up?"

"I'd bet my life they are."

"They better be because you just did bet your life." They had some coffee and discussed the best way to whack Georgie Z. "When this is done, you must step in and tell everyone that Georgie set up Vladimir's hit and that you are rightfully taking the Brotherhood back. There will be no payments to Boris, and from now on, the twenty-five percent Boris was supposed to get comes to us." They finished their coffees, and Mike walked out with Paul. The shooters relaxed and held their positions.

"I'll call you real soon," Mike told Paul, and they went their separate ways.

***

Danny East, Nicky Black, and Johnny Angel got into Johnny's new Cadillac S.T.S. As soon as the car started, the oldies' music came to life. Dion singing "The Majestic" filled the air. Johnny smiled and said, "This X.M. radio is great. I got a 50s station, a 60s station, a twenty-four-hour Elvis station, and a Sinatra station. What more could a man ask for?" Johnny cranked the music up so they could talk as they drove, just in case the car was bugged. With the music blasting, whoever was listening would not be able to hear what was being said. "We need to find Uncle Lenny."

"How do we do that?" Nick asked.

"I don't know, but we have to try. He's got no family besides my mom. They were always close, but he just disappeared. Nobody can find him. Can we hire a private detective?"

"The problem with that," Danny said, "is once they find out who we wanna find, they won't take the case."

"What if we convince them that we only want the money? The son of a bitch is gonna die soon anyway. We don't need to kill him."

"Okay," Nicky said, "I'll work on it. I'll try to find a P.I. who needs the work."

Johnny nodded his head. He had loved his Uncle Lenny all his life, and then the man goes bad. To make matters worse, he took off with a lot of money that did not belong to him. He had become a thorn in Johnny's side as well as an embarrassment to The Family. He had to be found and then lost for good.

"I've got someone in the phone company. Maybe I can track all the calls that came into your mom's house. That okay with you?" Nicky asked from the backseat.

"Do it," was all Johnny said. He then turned his attention back to Danny. "I need you to go see everyone in our crew and let them know from now on they'll be dealing with you when we all meet. If anyone needs to talk directly to me, they have to go through you." As Johnny drove, he glanced over to Danny sitting beside him.

Danny made a face. "You think that might insult some of our guys?"

"I don't give a fuck. That's the way it's gonna be. I'll say hello to everyone, but they discuss business with you, and then you talk with me. When you talk with the others, you make sure you never use my name. Capisce?"

Danny knew there was no sense in arguing. He just nodded his head and replied, "Si, capisco."

"In fact," Johnny continued, "if anyone is caught on tape saying my name, they'll get whacked. Make sure everyone understands that. Their life depends on it."

***

The shrimp in chili sauce was good. In fact, Lee thought it was the best he had ever had. He savored every bite as his sister chatted away. Once in a while, he nodded his head to make it look like he was paying attention, but he really did not want any part of this conversation. Sing May Chang was a beautiful woman, and time seemed to be very kind to her. She had the exact figure now at thirty-five as when she was seventeen. Her skin was as smooth and tight as she was in her youthful years. She could easily pass for twenty-one.

"Meng Chang! You are not listening to me."

"I'm trying to enjoy my meal, but you will not allow such a small pleasure, will you?"

"I'm serious. I want you to bring Johnny to my house for dinner."

"Sing, he is one of my dearest friends, and you want me to walk him into a trap."

She gasped, placing her hand over her heart. "A trap! You are calling me a trap!?" Sing had been in love with Johnny since she was twelve years old. She had fantasized about being his wife even when she was married to her ex-husband. She'd pretend it was Johnny coming home to her instead of him. Now that she was single and he was out of prison, she was determined to accomplish her mission.

"How could you say such a thing?"

He bit into the last jumbo shrimp and chewed it carefully, not wanting the exquisite pleasure of his palate to subside. His sister was getting on his last nerve, but he did not want to offend her. "I'm sorry, Sing, I did not mean it like that, but you are putting me in a very precarious situation here. I will tell Johnny you want to make dinner for him and the rest is up to you. I will not tag along and pretend I don't know what motives you have. Johnny is a big boy, and he can handle himself."

Sing smiled. That was the best deal she would get from her brother, and it was okay with her. She closed her eyes and pictured herself alone with Johnny in her apartment.

"So this is what you wanted to have lunch for? I thought you said you needed to talk with me, that it was important?"

"What could be more important?" she asked in all earnestness as she smoothed down her jet-black hair.

Lee just shook his head. "Aren't you a little old to be having a high school crush?"

She loved her brother, but he just did not get it and never would. Sing smiled and replied, "Nope!"

CHAPTER EIGHTEEN

It was another sweltering day in the city. Georgie Z drank the coffee that his wife had fixed for him. She was talking away about some anniversary party this coming weekend they had to go to. He was not looking forward to going, but he knew there was no escaping it. Getting up to go, he needed to be at the clubhouse to meet the crew. He was short with her and felt slightly guilty while she complained as he was leaving. If Georgie knew that these were his last few minutes alive, he surely would have been more kind. He really did love his wife; he just was not in the mood to hear all this chatter so early in the morning.

As he left the house, the heat hit him. He could see the heat waves bouncing off the concrete. The blacktop jungle's humidity was choking him. It was so thick Georgie thought he could slice it with a knife. He walked down the street to where he parked last night. As he approached the car, he noticed he had a flat tire. He looked around to see if there were any of the neighborhood kids that could change his tire. The usually busy streets were quiet, and Georgie realized the kids were finishing their last day of school. Oh well, he thought as he popped the trunk and started digging for his spare. He never noticed the two men that came up behind him until it was too late. They shot him six times, and as he fell forward into the trunk of his car, he realized he fell for the 'old flat tire' trick. How could I have been so stupid, he wondered.

Georgie's last thought was about the anniversary party this weekend, the one, his wife, wouldn't stop talking about—the one he would never get to go to. Little Mike was parked at the end of the block, watching the hit take place. He smiled as he drove off, thinking he'd like to do the same to that fucking Johnny Angel. Someday, he promised himself, *someday.*

***

Luis laughed as he swung the baseball bat again. It smashed into the side of his prey, breaking two of his ribs. John John was a runner for Raul Romero, the Dominican street boss in Washington Heights. Luis Almerez was the Puerto Rican street boss, and he was tired of dealing with the damn Dominicans. They were always stepping on Luis's territory, and he was not going to let that slide anymore. His men caught John John early in the morning selling dope on one of their blocks. Now, he would pay for it. Luis's ruthlessness was legendary. His nickname "Crazy Lou" was certainly well-earned. He stepped away and stared down at the bloodied body.

"The piece of shit is still breathing," he said in disgust. He sat down and lit a cigarette. "I have a good idea," he told his men. "We'll make it look like Yankee, and his crew did this. Give him the famous Colombian necktie and leave him in one of Raul's blocks. Let the Dominicans and the Colombians kill each other. Then we'll step in and finish off whoever is left."

In the late seventies, the Colombians were notorious for slitting their victim's throat, then cutting his tongue and pulling it down through the slit in their throat—the Colombian necktie. He watched as his men carried out his order. When they were done, he stood over the body. "Ah, that is disgusting! Take this poor bastard away." As they removed the defiled, mangled body, he thought about the consequences of starting a war. Fuck it, this barrio was too small for the Dominicans, Colombians, and Puerto Ricans. It was time the Puerto Ricans took control. After all, they were here first.

War was inevitable. Raul and Yankee had formed a bond, and it was only a matter of time before Raul made a move on him, and Yankee would take his back. Luis was too smart for them. He was a move ahead of those fools. Yankee was supposed to be neutral, an impartial judge, but Raul had been forging an alliance there. Now Yankee was no longer unbiased. Luis saw the whole movie building, and he was determined to drive a wedge between the two ethnic factions. This was a perfect plan killing two birds with one stone. Two birds with one stone? Suddenly, he realized how funny that expression sounded. Luis laughed good and hard. Two birds! Like killing two enemies with one bullet.

Johnny walked into the clubhouse in Harlem. s usual, Danny and Nick were arguing over a game of gin rummy. Johnny shook his head and made his way toward the coffee pot. Charlie Ponz, Joe Bats, and Danny's brother Gino were all there too. Gino was telling a story about a guy who hit the lottery for three million dollars. "He calls his wife and says, 'Honey, pack your bags. I just hit the lotto!' And then the wife says, 'Oh, God, that's great! Should I pack for winter or summer?' The husband says, 'I don't give a shit, just be gone by the time I get home.'" Everyone cracked up.

After Nick and Danny finished arguing, Danny paid Nick for losing once again. He caught Johnny's eye, motioning for him to walk outside. They started walking up the block, and Johnny said, "Do you ever win?"

"The guy's got unbelievable luck when it comes to knock-rummy."

"Danny," Johnny said in a serious tone, "luck would be the beats you for a few months straight. He's been beating you at knock rummy for thirty fucking years. That is not about luck."

"Fuck the both of yous. I need to report to you, not listen to a lecture on gin rummy."

"Well, go ahead and report then." Johnny held in his laughter. The two of them had been cursing each other out since they were kids. Johnny didn't expect that to change just because he now outranked Danny.

"We got two guys that need to get straightened out. Joey Bats and Gino are both up for it."

"Did they do a piece of work yet?" Johnny asked, referring to a hit. Each member was required to take part in a murder before they could qualify for induction into the family. It's called "making your bones."

Most families today did not keep up with the old tradition, but the Harlem crew did. Under Johnny's leadership, they would keep the old ways alive. It was a good way to flush out the rats, and it bound all the made guys to one another.

"They were both with me for Frankie Nat. Joey helped Charlie remove the body, and then Gino helped get rid of it."

"Why didn't they do it?"

"Gino was supposed to, but I didn't want anything to go wrong, so I took care of it myself. They're both ready, John. Ralphie already passed their names around. They're good to go."

"Okay, I'll look into it. What else?"

"Old man Paulie has got some professor from the college into him for a hundred G's. The guy ain't paying, so he wants some muscle to go over and collect for him.

He's too old to be doing that kind of shit. Who should I give that to?"

"Give it to Gino and Bats. The guy is a professor, so they should be able to appeal to his intellect."

"How so?" Danny asked, not sure how Johnny wanted this handled.

"He's a professor, Danny. He's got brains. Ask him if he realizes how hard it is to walk with two broken kneecaps."

"Gotcha. The next thing is Charlie's poker game. Patty from the Bronx came to see Charlie and told him that Ralphie had him in for a piece of the game, and now that Ralphie was gone, he'd be around every week for his share."

"Patty with the Lucchese Family had a piece of Charlie's poker game?" "That's what he's claiming. He said he helped Ralphie start the game thirty years ago and has always gotten a piece, but Charlie doesn't know anything about it. How do you want me to handle that?"

"That's the biggest poker game in the city, and it brings in lots of dough for us. Go up to the Bronx and see Patty. Ask him how much was he getting, and then ask Charlie how much was he kicking up to Ralphie."

"I already asked Charlie what he was giving Ralphie. Two grand a week, he said. He also said Patty told him the games been on record since it started, so he must be telling the truth."

"Then Patty couldn't have been getting more than five hundred a week from Ralphie. That's your limit. Go see him and make it right. Tell him to send some players down to pump the game up."

"Shit, Johnny, that game runs three tables a night and five on the weekends. It don't need no pumping up."

"Just take care of it, would ya? Don't make mountains out of molehills. We got more important shit to worry about. You and Nicky, meet me downtown tonight. We need to get on top of a couple of things."

CHAPTER NINETEEN

The Baltic was a new restaurant that had just opened last week. Boris had backed a young couple and financed the whole thing. It was a first-class, fine dining establishment with authentic Russian cuisine. The husband and wife both cooked and ran the place. The back of the restaurant held a huge banquet room, and that was precisely where Boris held tonight's meeting.

The top echelon of the Bratva had gathered together. Boris was pacing around the room. He did not anticipate that someone would challenge Georgie and make a move on him. Now this son of a bitch Paul was running the show, and poor Georgie was dead. Boris knew that Paul was Little Mike's puppet. He also realized that as long as Little Mike was around, he would always have his hands in the Brotherhood. Russian Paul had sent a message over that he was now in charge, and they would not be cutting The Izmaylovskaya Gang in on their take of anything. Paul left the door open for peace by pointing out that The Izmaylovskaya was never part of their Brotherhood, but they wished them well and hoped that peace would suffice, but they needed to keep their brotherhoods separate.

"Ivan, you go to Russian Paul, explain to him that Vladimir made a move on us, we countered, and we came out victorious. As a result of that, we should be compensated because we agreed with Georgie not to pursue the conflict. We could have kept attacking, but we did not. See what he says about that."

Ivan nodded his head. "Okay, boss," was all he replied.

"Our next problem is the main one. Little Mike." Boris looked at each of his men, trying to read their thoughts. "He needs to go, but we must be very careful about this. Any thoughts?"

Maxim said, "Why don't we put a kilo of dope in his car and let the police take him down. Or maybe we can hire some blacks to take him out?"

"I like your first thought," Boris said. "We can't take a chance on using people outside the Brotherhood—that might backfire on us. Let's discuss this idea about setting him up with some dope."

Maxim cleared his throat and said, "It's easy. We take a kilo of dope and put it under the front passenger seat. We tip off a cop. They pull him over and bust him. And it's Bye-bye, Little Mike."

"He's gonna know he was set up," Boris said with a good deal of concern.

Ivan jumped into the conversation for the first time. "Why don't we just whack him and make him disappear? They won't know he's dead. They'll think he just took off."

"He's a made guy. He has to report. He just can't take off without checking in. No, that won't work, but I like the idea of setting him up. The problem is that he'll eventually figure out it was us, and we'll have a war on our hands."

"Let's just whack him," Ivan said again. "We can make it look like it was about something else."

"Like what kind of something else?" Boris asked.

"I don't know," Ivan confessed.

"But it was your idea to make it look like something else. What something else are you talking about?" Boris pressed.

"I don't know," Ivan said, waving his hand in the air, wishing he had kept his mouth shut. "I can kill him, and you can come up with the story."

"Anybody in this room can kill him. The more important thing is to not be the ones who looked like we killed him."

"Well, that's too complicated for me."

Boris shook his head and made a face. "Okay, let's everybody just think about that, and we'll talk again tomorrow." When everyone was gone, Boris sat there and thought about the whole deal. Anyway, he looked at the scenario, it came back to getting rid of Little Mike. He thought about talking to Johnny, but he knew Johnny would never okay a hit on Mike because he was a made guy. But there was one thing he was sure about… Little Mike was a problem that had to be removed, one way or another. The sooner, the better.

***

One hundred and fourteen bullets were fired in the latest conflict between the drug cartels. Five people were dead, including two innocent bystanders and a police officer. Yankee was watching the news coming out of the Mexican border town of Juarez near El Paso, Texas. He shook his head in frustration. Did these foolish Mexicans not realize the ramifications of that useless violence? This was surely going to have a bad effect on business. It was time for Yankee to take control of the Mexican problem. They were getting way too big for their britches and way too sloppy for Yankee's taste. He hoped his people would agree with that.

Tito knocked on the door and said, "Raul is here, and he seems very upset." "Send him in." Raul came into the office with Tito behind him. They shook hands, and as Raul sat down across from him, he said, "It seems lately all I have is bad news for you." Yankee did not reply, so Raul continued. "That fucking Crazy Lou went too far this time. He killed John John and tried to make it look like you did it." Raul explained the whole thing to Yankee, who just sat there in silence.

Yankee clasped his hands together and tapped his index fingers as he thought about what he was just told. After a moment of reflection, he came to a decision. Crazy Lou had gone too far. "I'm leaving for Bogota in the morning. I won't be back for a couple of weeks. It would be a perfect time to clean the house around here. If you need some capable men, see Tito while I'm gone."

Raul smiled. He wasn't sure if Yankee would have been okay with this. Raul had already made up his mind to take Crazy Lou out regardless of how Yankee felt, so he was glad that Yankee agreed. He nodded and said, "I think if we remove Lou, the rest of those guys would be willing to make peace. If not, we'll kill them too."

"They need to understand that even if John John was on their turf, the right move was to come to you with it, not take matters into their own hands. When I get back, I will call a meeting to make sure everyone understands the rules. In the meantime, you are careful. They don't call him Crazy Lou for nothing. He's a loose cannon. He's probably plotting his next move already."

Raul smiled again, even bigger this time. "And I am not the boss of my gang without good reason." He got up, shook Yankee's hand, and said, "Have a good trip. Things will be different when you get back."

When Raul left, Yankee turned to Tito. "Make sure things don't get too crazy while I'm gone—and be careful. I don't trust this Crazy Lou. I wouldn't put it past him to make a move on any of us. Tell everyone to be on alert. I'm sure Raul can handle this, but if it seems like trouble, send the troops out and finish this Crazy Lou off."

***

The club was packed with a line out the door and halfway down the block. Apollo, Cecil, and Ray ignored the line and went directly to the front door. Everyone entering the club had to pass through a metal detector, except, of course, for Apollo and his men. He loved seeing such a thriving business, especially since he was a silent partner. He never acted like he owned the place. He always seemed to be a regular V.I.P. customer, even paying his tabs at the end of the night. Most people knew right away who the real boss was because of how the owner doted on him whenever he came around. There were so many beautiful women there, but right now, he paid them no mind. Apollo and his crew sat at his usual booth, and the waitress came over to take their order. She was new and had a fantastic smile.

"Hello, gentlemen. What can I get you?"

"You new here?" Apollo asked, already knowing that she was.

"First night," she replied with that knock-out smile.

"What's your name?"

"Micki."

"Well, nice to meet you, Nikki."

"That's Micki with an 'M.' M-i-c-k-I," she spelled out for him with extra emphasis on the 'I.'

Apollo laughed. "Okay, M-i-c-k-I," he said, spelling it back to her. "Nice to meet you."

"Nice to know you're a good speller. Now, what can I get you guys to drink?"

"Oh, spunky. I like that." Apollo ordered drinks for the three of them. "Get yourself one and join us."

"I can't drink while I'm working but thank you anyway." She smiled and walked off toward the bar. There seemed to be a little more shake in her walk after their interaction.

Apollo laughed, shook his head, and said, "Byebye, Tamika. Hello Micki."

Donald, the owner, came by to say hello.

"The new girl Micki," Apollo said, not even looking at Donald. "Tell her to get a drink and come sit with us for a few minutes."

"Right away," Donald said, all smiles, and walked off. A minute later, Micki was back with their drinks and one for herself.

"You got a little clout, I see. Cheers," she said, holding her glass up.

"I'm just a good customer, and Donald knows how to take care of his regulars."

"Yeah, I'll bet," she said as she took a sip and smiled. He was obviously more than a good customer. This was the guy, no doubt about it.

CHAPTER TWENTY

Theresa laughed as she watched Johnny trying to keep up with Angel. The child was full of energy, running around the petting zoo in Central Park. She was fascinated with the animals as she went from one pen to the next. Johnny caught up with her trying to feed the llama with a hand full of corn. It had been a good day Theresa thought as she watched Johnny and Angel get to know one another. Johnny had spent the whole day with them, starting with breakfast at the Second Avenue Diner, then bowling, shopping, and now the small petting zoo in Central Park.

She watched him answer his cell phone and motion for her to come over. She could tell by the look on his face that the day was about to end. Damn cell phones. Johnny was having a great time with his daughter. When his phone rang, he almost did not answer it. He couldn't make out the number without his reading glasses on so he just answered it anyway. "Hello."

"I'm glad you answered," Uncle Lenny said. "Do you hate me?"

Johnny was shocked. Here he was in the middle of the zoo, with his steady girlfriend and his daughter, having a normal day—almost normal— until he heard from his missing uncle-turned-rat, Lenny. He walked off by himself. He wasn't sure how to respond. "Why'd you do it, Unc?"

"I didn't wanna die in the joint." "But that's what happens to guys like us. We don't die at home in our sleep very often. So now you're gonna die alone. Which is worse?"

"I gave my life to this thing of ours Johnny, and you know that. It ain't like it used to be. When my skipper flipped and was gonna tell on me, I thought 'that's fucked up. You ordered me to kill all these people and now you're gonna tell on me about them?' If I got caught with a body I would've kept my mouth shut and died in the joint—but I just couldn't swallow going this way."

"So you called me for what, to justify your betrayal? You got a sour deal. So what? That's no excuse."

"No, Johnny. I just wanted to know if you hate me."

Johnny shook his head. "I don't hate you Unc. I'm just really disappointed in you. I'd still kill you in a minute if I saw you."

"I know you would and I understand that. I just wanted to know if you hated me."

"Why did you take all that money? You know that made matters even worse, like pouring salt on the wound."

Lenny laughed on the other end of the line. "Exactly," he said.

"So what are you gonna do with all that cash? You're too damn old to enjoy it." Johnny had stopped a distance from Theresa and Angel. He stood there listening to Uncle Lenny and watching his daughter. All he could think of was What a crazy life we lead.

"You, your mother, sister and nephew are the only family I got, John. The money is yours. I took some to last me but most of it is waiting for you."

"I hope you're not waiting for me to say thanks."

"No. I don't want anything from you, Johnny Angel. You'll find the money in your mom's basement in the wall behind the furnace. Try and remember the good times, kid. Don't dwell on the negative."

There was a brief pause on the line. "I do have one favor to ask…"

"I'm listening," replied Johnny.

"I'd like to be buried next to my mother and father."

"Yeah, well don't expect a big funeral."

"Take care, Johnny Angel. Watch out for all the rats around you." And with that, Lenny hung up.

Johnny looked at the phone for a minute and shook his head. He thought about the phone call. Lenny must have figured Johnny would try and find him. Maybe he thought he could appease Johnny with the money and Johnny would not bother to look for him. To Johnny, this was way beyond the money—it was a matter of honor. He walked back over to Theresa. "What'd you say we take Angel up to see my mother?" Theresa looked up and smiled. She thought he was going to tell her he had to go out. She was beaming. "What a great idea!" she exclaimed.

"Yeah." Johnny laughed. "It's a million-dollar idea. Come on, let's go."

***

Luis Almerez was a cautious man. Paranoid was more like it. His motto was, 'It's better to be paranoid than right'. When he stepped out of a building or a car, he always had a hand in his pocket holding a pistol. When he was at home, the gun rested right next to him at all times. He had a gun in every room. He even had a gun wrapped in a plastic bag in the shower. His bodyguards that were always with him also had their fingers on the trigger. Ready to get down at all times. Luis liked to party. He was always high on coke. If he's awake, he was using. Most people start their day with a nice cup of coffee. Luis began his day with a few good lines. He didn't spend time talking with most of his customers but there were a few that he sat with, always turning them on to some lines.

Dominick "Chilly" Chilente was Luis's favorite customer. He bought about half a key a week, which was not big time but Dom was an Italian gangster. Luis was fascinated with the mafia so when he told Luis that his boss wanted to meet with him, Luis was ecstatic. Little Mike DeStaffino was a well-known name to Luis.

"It's a pleasure to meet you, sir," Luis said.

"Sit," Mike replied, gesturing with his hand to an empty seat next to him. They were in a bar in the Bronx. It was a quiet little hole-in-the-wall place, a neighborhood joint that opened at ten in the morning, full by eleven. Like morning drinkers all over the city, each guy had his regular stool, determined to spend the day—or as much of it as possible—perched, swimming in memories.

Mike operated his bookmaking business from there. "What can we get you to drink?"

"A beer is good." Mike nodded his head and the waitress immediately came over. He ordered a round for everyone. Turning his attention back to Luis, he said, "Chilly tells me you're boxed in over there in your neighborhood."

Luis laughed and bragged about changing that. "Well, not for long. I just sent a message a couple of days ago. That should stir things up."

"Well, maybe we can help each other out. I've got an interest in someone that you don't know who happens to be very close to this Yankee character. I want to rip this piece of shit's heart out, but I can't do that. Not directly anyway. So the next best thing would be to weaken his position by taking Yankee out."

"Yankee left for Colombia. He's usually gone for a few weeks."

"That's fine, it gives us time to plan."

"You know the Bellohauntos Cartel is behind Yankee one hundred percent. They will come at you big time." Mike had met hundreds of people over the years that were fascinated with the mafia, wanting to impress him. He pegged Luis for being another one, another wannabe wiseguy with a gun.

He had a slight smirk that was not unnoticed by Luis when he asked, "Are you afraid of them?" Luis shook his finger wildly in the air.

"Luis Almerez is not afraid of anyone," he said defensively. "But to start a war with these people, there must be something big in it for me."

"The most important thing is honor, don't you agree?" Mike knew exactly how to play him.

"Yes, but honor can't buy guns."

"It can. I'll supply you with a few good men. The payoff for you would be control of your neighborhood."

"That all sounds good Mike but this cartel is huge. They'll just keep sending hit squads."

Mike smiled. He turned to Chilly and pointing at Luis, he said, "I like this guy." The truth was Mike didn't care about Luis at all. He was just an instrument to be used. Turning back to Luis, he smiled and held his hand out. "Think about how we can do this and we'll talk again next week. Remember, Luis, that the strength of a man is not about what he can pick up but rather in what he can defend and protect. I'll have Chilly call you."

Luis stood up and shook his hand and then Chilly's. He was feeling ten feet tall when he left the meeting with Little Mike. Sitting down with the mafia was the biggest accomplishment of his life. He felt like he had arrived. He was very impressed with Little Mike. When they would meet next week, Luis was determined to deliver what Mike wanted. This gangster business had just hit a new plateau. Things were looking up for him.

When Luis was gone, Mike looked at Chilly and said, "Okay, we got the Russian thing under control. Hopefully, this fool will join the cause. Now we need to figure a way to get to the blacks in Harlem that Johnny Angel has with him."

Chilly made a face and said, "That shouldn't be too hard. We can call a sit-down over the numbers and gambling and claim it belongs to us. When they show for the meet, we'll whack them."

"Let me think about that. Johnny's power comes from the Russians, the blacks, the Chinese and the Colombians. There's no way to get into the Chinese crew. They don't deal with us at all—only Johnny. We'll have to pass on that part. But if we can take out Yankee and that spook in Harlem, and we crush the rest of the Russian crew, Johnny's position would weaken considerably."

"And with all that going on," Chilly began, "no one would finger us if Johnny got whacked in the process." Little Mike smiled.

"Now that is a brilliant idea, Chilly. Good thinking. Let's make this happen."

CHAPTER TWENTY-ONE

The meal was perfect. She could tell how much Johnny enjoyed it. "Some more tea, Johnny?" she asked.

"Sing May Chang, that was a fantastic dinner. I didn't know you were such a great cook," he answered as he wiped his mouth.

"Is it not correct that the way to a man's heart is through his stomach?"

Johnny laughed. "That's what the Italians say. And yes, I'll have one more cup of tea."

She got up and poured him a fresh cup of tea. When she laid the pot down on the table, she started massaging his shoulders. Johnny responded with a pleasant sigh.

"Oh, Sing, you better watch it. I'm gonna have to take a nap if you don't stop that." "I will fix the bed for you to lie down and relax before you have to run out to your busy world."

"Anything to get me in bed," he said jokingly.

"Yes, Johnny, anything," she replied and leaned over his shoulder to kiss him. Johnny was caught off-guard and had to stop himself before he was lost in the kiss and victimized by lust.

Sing was a beautiful woman, but she was Lee's sister. He pulled away from her. "Sing, don't get me started." She was not willing to back down. "I have waited my whole life to get you started, Johnny Angel. I will not give up now." She reached down and kissed him again, and this time, he did not deny her. Johnny stood up, turned around, and put his arms around her. He kissed her back passionately.

She felt good in his arms. Lee had warned him that Sing was trying to trap him with dinner. He had laughed and agreed anyway. Releasing his embrace, Johnny said, "Sing, you don't wanna get mixed up with a guy like me."

"I want to more than anything I have ever wanted," she said as she batted her eyes up at him.

"I'm not dependable in relationships."

"I do not care."

"I'm never around—always busy."

"I do not care."

"I'm not the marrying kind. You know, wife and kids ain't my speed."

"I do not care."

He thought he might as well get brutally honest. "Sing, I've got a lady friend that I stay with."

"I do not care. Now you have two lady friends."
He had no comeback for that one. Johnny picked her up
and carried her to the bedroom. They made fierce, wild
love until they both exploded in ecstasy. They lay there
for a few minutes, and Sing rolled over and started
kissing him lightly on the lips, face, and neck. She trailed
her way down his chest until she had him in her mouth.
Johnny was erect again, and they made love again for the
next thirty minutes.

He turned over onto his stomach, and Sing started
massaging his back. She said, "That was fantastic,
Johnny. Like I always knew it would be." The only reply
was a slight snore. Johnny was fast asleep.

***

"This is my brother Jerome. Jerome, this is Apollo." The
two men shook hands. This was the fourth straight night
Apollo had taken Micki out. She invited him in to meet
her brother, who she lived with.

"Can I get you something to drink?" Jerome asked.

"No thanks, I can't stay. I just wanted to say hi. It
was nice meeting you."

"You too, take care." Micki kissed him goodbye
and walked him to the door.

When he was gone, she turned back to Jerome. "I
don't think I can do this."

Jerome shook his head. "Don't get cold feet on us now, Micki. Don't forget the drug charge hanging over your head. It's this or twenty years in the big house for you and Grandma."

She fought back the tears and pleaded. "You know my grandmother didn't even know the dope was in the house. That's rotten of you.

And Apollo's not stupid. He's not going to tell me anything or do anything in front of me."

"We don't expect him to. Your job is to hook me up with him. That may take some time. We might be undercover for a year or more, but we're going to do this. Once you get in tight with him, he'll be glad to help out your big brother. Look, Micki, if it'll make you feel any better, we don't really give a shit about Apollo. We want Johnny Angel. If we catch Apollo right, where he's facing life, he'll give us Johnny Angel, and that's what this whole operation is about."

"I haven't met Johnny Angel or even heard his name yet."

"You will trust me. Tell Apollo you want to go eat Italian food. That might speed things up some."

"This is the hardest thing I've ever had to do," she said in a shaky voice. Her hands trembled as she spoke.

"It's easier than doing twenty years. Just remember that. And you don't want us putting the cuffs on Grandma, do you? When this is done, the Bureau will relocate you, and you'll be free with a brand-new start in life. It's a good deal, Micki. Just stick with it."

Jerome sat down when she went to her room and wrote out his report. This case was going to rocket him up the ladder. The powers that be would be forced to take a serious look at his work. After seven years as an F.B.I. agent, he finally felt like he was doing something big time. He dated the paper and noted the time, and wrote his first meaningful entry. "Made contact with Mark Owens, a.k.a. Apollo."

***

Danny threw the seven clubs. Nicky picked it up, shuffled his hand around, and said, "Gin," with a big ol' smile.

Danny threw the remaining cards in the air. "I can't believe how lucky you are!"

"What lucky? You threw me two sevens. You're not paying attention today. Where's your head at?" Nicky totaled the score. "That's two eighty-five you owe me."

Danny reached into his pocket, put the money on the table, and got up. He walked over to the coffeepot and poured himself a cup. He was still shaking his head when Johnny walked in. The first thing Johnny noticed was the cards strewn across the floor. Secondly, he saw Nicky counting the money and then Danny talking to himself at the coffeepot.

Johnny laughed and shook his head. "Let me guess," he said to Danny, "the son-of-a-bitch got lucky, right?"

Danny nodded. "It's fucking unbelievable, ain't it, John. The guy got more luck than Charlie Sheen's got hookers."

"Yeah," Johnny replied, still smiling. "It's unbelievable. What's going on?"

Danny motioned for the door and pointed to Nicky. "Can he come?" Johnny nodded, and the three men walked outside. They started walking up the block, and Danny said, "A few things. First off, Nicky wasn't able to find out anything about Uncle Lenny. The calls were patched through the F.B.I.'s switchboard. No telling where they came from."

"What if he called from a cell phone?" Johnny asked.

Nicky shook his head. "It doesn't matter if he gets patched through. We can't know where they're coming from."

"You think the Feds would patch him through to me?"

"Highly unlikely. That would be a breach of security, I'm sure."

"Well, he called me yesterday." Johnny waited for their reactions. Danny and Nicky both had looks of shock on their faces.

"What'd he say?" Danny asked.

"Just wanted to explain why he did what he did and wanted to know if I hated him."

"What was his explanation?"

"He said his skipper was gonna give him up and he couldn't swallow going away like that."

"What about the money? Did you ask him about the money?"

Johnny smiled. "Of course, I did. He swears he didn't take it. Said someone else glommed it up and was blaming him for it." Johnny saw no need to tell them about the money Lenny had directed him to at his mom's house. There were almost a million and a half there. Johnny had no intention of sharing it. "We need to find him. Nicky, see if you can trace my cell phone and find out where that call came from."

Nicky nodded his head. "Right," was all he said.

"Next thing," Danny said, "is old man Sully. Seems he ran a scam on some guys connected to Sonny

173

Cap downtown. Took them for about fifty G's. Sonny sent word he wanted to talk with you unofficially, off the record."

"Did you talk to Sully?"

Danny laughed. "If you wanna call it that. That old fucker went right to 'let's start a war with the Gambinos.' He said those guys weren't with anybody, and they ran to Sonny for help now, after the fact. He said to tell you the money's gone, so he can't give any back."

Johnny laughed too. "You gotta love that old man. He's the best. He's so smooth he can sell a bag of shit to the smartest guy in the world. You remember working with him when we were kids?"

Danny and Nicky both smiled, remembering the old days with Sully. Nicky chimed in, "Ralphie always said besides us, no one got in more trouble than old man Sully. I guess it's our turn to look after him."

Johnny looked at his watch. "Eight o'clock on Friday night. You know Sonny's playing cards downtown. I'll go by and see him. It'll be easier if I bug him in the middle of a card game. He'll want to get back to the table, so he'll be easier to deal with. All right, anything else?"

Nicky made a hand gesture and shook his head no.

Danny nodded. "Yeah, one more thing. When we gonna straighten out our guys?"

"As soon as they open the books. There's a batch of about eight guys waiting, so it should be soon. Gino will replace Ralphie, so he's for sure. We'll have to see about the rest. Okay. I'm going downtown to see Sonny." Johnny walked off, heading for the next fire to put out. He shook his head. In this life, there was always something happening—never a dull moment. He wondered what would come next.

CHAPTER TWENTY-TWO

In the cab to Mulberry Street in Little Italy, Johnny thought about his old friend Sonny Caparelli. They had been friends for many years, though it didn't start out that way. Sonny Cap, as he was commonly known, was a real gangster—an old-fashioned street guy. Johnny smiled as he remembered way back in his teens and the fight he had with Sonny. To this very day, he never had a tougher fight in his life, and he believed Sonny would say the same. It was thirty years ago, give or take. The downtown bar was packed and loud. Johnny, Nicky, and Danny were talking to a few girls. Everyone in the bar was underage. In those days, it was common for sixteen and seventeen-year-olds to drink in bars. The legal age was eighteen back then. Half the kids were from East Harlem and the other half from Mulberry Street. Almost all were Italian. Their parents were from Southern Italy: Naples, Sicily, Abruzzi, all the places the Northern Italians looked down on. These were tough kids—some tougher than others.

Sonny was making his way to the bathroom and squeezed past Johnny's group. He put his hand on the girl's butt that Johnny was talking to, and after some words, Sonny hit Johnny. Both kids were about the same in weight and height. They fought from the back of the bar to the front door and outside onto the street. The amazing thing was it did not turn into a giant brawl. Everybody had the same attitude that it was an even fight, so they let them duke it out.

Johnny was beating the shit out of Sonny, and Sonny was beating the shit out of Johnny. It was the longest, best fight anyone there had ever seen. At one point, Sonny grabbed Johnny in a headlock as they both smashed over the hood of a car. Somehow Johnny had reversed it, and they lay on the street, both holding on to each other and still throwing punches.

"Had enough yet?" Sonny asked.

"Nah…you?" replied Johnny.

"I could use a fucking drink!" Sonny said.

"Me too," replied Johnny. They let go of each other and helped one another up. The fight was almost twenty minutes of non-stop slugging. The crowd applauded as they all went back inside. They had been friends ever since. To this day, people talk about the fight between Sonny Cap and Johnny Angel, two men whose lives would crisscross and intersect as they rose up the ladder of the Mafia. Though Johnny had not seen Sonny since he got out, he heard about Sonny getting made. Sonny's brother Blackie Danone was the boss of the Gambino family. There had been a short war for control of the family, and Sonny had been shot. He recovered, and Blackie won the struggle for the family.

Once Sonny was well enough for retribution, he killed the guy who shot him. Because that guy was a made man and Sonny was not, Blackie insisted that Sonny get made so he would be protected. Sonny had always resisted being made because he didn't want to be accountable to anyone and have all kinds of rules he had to live by—but Blackie left him no choice. The rules of the street were simple: you touch a mad guy. You die, so Blackie hurried up and had the ceremony so he could claim Sonny was already made when the fight happened—and it was just two made guys fighting each other. That was still not kosher, but it wouldn't end with Sonny being killed. Since then, Blackie had promoted him to captain. And now, Sonny had sent word to him that he wanted to talk off the record.

Because of the bond the two men had, that was possible. Otherwise, if the two of them wanted to talk, any meeting would have to be a big sit-down. As he got out of the cab, Johnny realized he was anxious to see his old friend. Sure enough, he found Sonny at a poker table. Everyone said hello, and Sonny got up and hugged him. They went to the back of the club to talk.

"You look good, Johnny. That time on vacation did you some good."

"Yeah, I worked on my tan. And you're getting fat, my friend."

"Yeah," Sonny laughed. "We're getting old but don't let this fool you," Sonny rubbed his belly. "I can still kick your ass."

It was Johnny's turn to laugh. "Still? 'Still' insinuates you once did."

"Yeah, well, forget that shit. I'd die if we went more than two minutes. That's why I just shoot the bastards today. Can't fight like when we were kids anymore."

"Shit, you couldn't fight then either." Both men laughed, and Sonny hugged Johnny again. They caught up with each other for a few minutes, and then Sonny said, "What are we gonna do about Old Sully? These guys he took for fifty large are with me."

"He told me to tell you he knows they weren't with you when he conned them."

"I ain't gonna try and bullshit the biggest bullshit artist in the world so tell him yes, that's true—but they're with me now."

"Come on, Sonny. You know I ain't gonna be able to get no money from Sully. You used to work for him too. Remember how hard it was to get our pay from that tight-ass old fuck?"

Sonny laughed. He truly loved Sully, and he respected Johnny as much as anyone around. "I have a solution that might work. Let him take these two meatballs on a score. Let them earn something back. They'll have to kick some this way, and we'll all be happy."

Johnny thought that was fair enough, but he pressed it anyway. "Sully's already happy."

"Yeah, but I ain't."

Good enough of an answer, Johnny thought. "Okay, I'll talk to him. Send my regards to Blackie and tell him I said congratulations."

"I'll do that. Take care, Johnny Angel. Watch out. There are bad guys everywhere. Good seeing you."

Leaving the card game where Sonny was, he had a private car take him up to the Bronx. He didn't feel like driving. Sully, like Sonny, would also be at a card game at this time on a Friday night. Johnny laughed. If he weren't running around for these two old friends, he'd be at a game himself. Armando Gullianni, a.k.a. Al Sullivan, a.k.a. Sully, was a soldier in the Genovese Family in Johnny's crew. Like many of the old-time Mafioso, Armando took an Irish name way back in the day because the Irish were much more established in the country than the Italians. And it always threw the police off if they were looking for a guy named Sullivan—they would not be in the Italian neighborhood. Most of the police were Irish, so if they thought they were looking for an Irishman, they wouldn't work as hard as if they knew the guy they wanted was Italian. Plus, they'd never look in the Italian neighborhood for an Irishman.

Sully was a street hustler. He ran every type of scam that mankind had ever heard of. He invented the T.V. scam that made millions of dollars over the years. They would call offices around the city, and the initial caller would make like he was the janitor of the building. He explained that today was his day off, and he was helping his brother, who was a supervisor on the docks at Macy's. Sully would then get on the phone and explain that they had a bunch of televisions and computers that didn't get shipped out. If they could pick them up today, he could give them a fantastic price. Sully was so good that he would convince people to get money from their family and friends and other workers there because they had to buy everything he had in order to make this deal work. They would give the phone number to a payphone of a bar or corner phone where they were working that day. The sucker would call them back, and they would answer saying "Macy's" and switch them back to Sully. Sully would have them come to the loading docks where a kid would come out to get their envelope. The kid would take the envelope and walk back to the docks, go through the door, and out the other side of the building, where Sully would pick him up. One day, his kid was no-showed for work, so Sully played all three phone parts and went out to get the envelope. He beat bookmakers in horse parlors with invisible ink. He ran phony card and dice games where the whole set-up was just to take one guy.

Sully was banned from every casino and racetrack in the country. Once, he fixed eight races in one night at Yonkers Raceway. Sully was a sharp dresser and big spender. He was a wheeler-dealer and lived a fast life. He gambled every day and every night. He could make five thousand in two minutes and lose it in one. Or the other way around. You never knew with Sully. All the young guys worked for Sully at one time or another, learning the ropes of the streets. All these years later, Johnny was his captain. As Johnny pulled up and entered the card game, he reminded himself that Al Sullivan was a legend and one of his idols.

Johnny took a seat next to Sully and watched as Sully bluffed a guy out of the game with nine high. The other guy had jacks showing. As Sully scooped the cash up with a big smile, he said,

"Come on, Johnny, join us. We got an empty seat." Johnny smiled.

"I thought you'd never ask. We need to talk later."

Sully nodded his head. "Later. Now, we play." Four hours later, Sully yawned. "I'm done," he stated. He and Johnny got up from the table. Johnny was up about seven hundred. Sully was ahead a lot more than that. "Looks like I brought you luck," Johnny said.

"Luck is just a third of the game, kid. You need balls and skill to win consistently."

They walked over to the coffee pot in the makeshift kitchen. "I talked with Sonny."

"And?"

"And you can imagine what he said."

"Those punks weren't with him when I took them." "He agrees with that." "So, case closed. Next problem."

"Next problem is these guys are with him now."

"And?" Johnny thought about the best way to say this. He knew if Sully thought he was being bullied, he would protest big time.

"Sonny said to tell you it would be nice if you could make him look good and cut these guys in on a score. They'd feel like they were getting paid back, and Sonny would earn, and we'd all be happy."

"I'm already happy."

Johnny laughed. "That's exactly what I told him."

"And?"

"And what? It's your call. Tell me what you're willing to do."

Sully was dying to say 'fuck them,' but in this case, he was dealing with old friends. They were being nice about the whole thing, asking for a favor rather than telling him what they wanted. "You're my skipper. What do you want me to do?"

Johnny shook his head. "No, no," he said, waving his hand. "You ain't putting this off on me. Your call."

"You know, you and Sonny, you guys are a lot alike. You could even pass for brothers. Didn't he whoop your ass when you were kids?"

Johnny laughed. He had to be on his toes with Sully at all times. He was trying to get Johnny upset, so Johnny would say 'fuck them' for him.

"No, Sully, he didn't whoop my ass, but he came damn close. Closer than anyone ever did."

"Well, I like both of you, so okay, tell him I'll do it. I don't know where these two meatballs could be of help, but I'll find something."

"Thanks, Sully. That's the right thing to do."

"If it's the right thing, why didn't you say so when I fucking asked you?"

Johnny hugged Sully and said, "Good night, pal."
He wasn't about to get into a debate with Sully Sullivan.

CHAPTER TWENTY-THREE

The two Dobermans sat straight up on either side of Boris. Erect at their sentinel positions, they made a very impressive statement. The warehouse was dimly lit with huge out-of-date furniture that looked like a throwback to the seventies.

The man on the other side of the desk was obviously nervous. "Please, Mr. Boris, I just need a little more time," he begged in a heavy Russian accent.

"How much do you owe?" Boris tapped his index fingers together.

The man looked down and replied, "Twenty-five thousand."

"How much more time are we talking about?" The man got his hopes up when he heard that question. He quickly raised his head. "Three more months."

"If you can't pay now, what's different three months from now?" Boris asked, tapping his fingers together faster. "I have money tied up that I cannot get to right yet. The money is guaranteed."

"The only thing guaranteed is that I will kill you if you don't pay me. I will grant you three extra months— but it'll cost you. You bring me forty thousand in ninety days, or I'm finished talking with you."

The man blew out a sigh of relief. He had not been sure if he was going to walk out of there ten minutes ago. At least not in one piece, he thought. "Thank you, Mr. Boris. Thank you very much. I will not let you down!" he said as he stood up and bowed toward him.

When the man left, Boris looked at Ivan and Maxim, who were standing next to the now-empty chair in case they were ordered to grab the man. "Is there anything else?"

Ivan brought out a small suitcase and placed it on the desk. "Four million," he said. "Four?" Boris asked. "I thought I had three?" "The other million belongs to me and Maxim. We want you to give it to Johnny from us too. It will be cheaper to do four rather than three. Is that correct?"

"I don't think so. It's a hundred and fifty thousand per million. Do you still want it taken care of?"

"How does that all work?" Maxim asked.

"I have no idea, Maxim. If I give this to Johnny, he will have three million, four hundred thousand legal investments. He will keep six hundred thousand for himself. How he does it is none of my business, nor should you be asking such questions."

"I'm only asking you," Maxim said defensively. "I would never ask Johnny." Boris nodded his understanding.

"You will need a name and social security number to go with the money. After it is washed, you will have your share in a legitimate investment. The money cannot be traced back to where it came from. In my book, that is worth every penny of the price we pay."

The two men nodded their consent and agreed to the percentage for Johnny.

"Good. I have to meet with him now. You can drive me. Bring the suitcase," he commanded. Traffic was heavy leaving Brooklyn and going into Manhattan. It was four-thirty by the time they reached the social club in Harlem. Boris knew better than to walk in there with a suitcase, so he told Ivan and Maxim to stay in the car with the money. When Boris entered the club, Johnny sent Danny out to the car. He jumped in and said, "Drop me a few blocks from here with the suitcase. Boris said he'll see you back in Brooklyn." The men did not question Danny and just drove off.

Back inside the clubhouse, Johnny said, "Let's have dinner, and then I'll have someone take you back to your place." Paulie the Zip was a Made guy in Johnny's crew. He had a nice Italian restaurant on Second Avenue and Eighty-Eighth Street. The Americans called the people born in Italy "Zips." Paulie was from Italy, so that's where his nickname came from.

He lit up when his captain walked through the door. It wasn't even six o'clock yet, but the place was filling up fast. Johnny turned to Paulie and said, "Paulie, this is a dear friend of mine, Boris. Boris, meet Paulie." The two men shook hands. "Any friend of Johnny Angel's is a friend of mine. Welcome."

"Paulie, sit and have a drink with us."

"I will, John. Let me get you guys something to pick on first." Paulie left and was back within a few minutes with a tray of antipasti. The three men sat around, drank, and talked about sports and the news. They laughed and joked about everything and nothing. When the meal came out, Paulie excused himself.

As soon as they were alone, Boris said, "We need to talk about that, Little Mike."

"What about him?" Johnny said, not really wanting to hear this.

"I know you're not gonna like this, but he's gotta go."

Johnny stopped eating. He looked at Boris like he was crazy. "You know I can't okay that."

"He's bad news, Johnny. He whacked Georgie and put Russian Paul in charge. That whole crew is rightfully mine now, not his. Where does this little piece of shit come off tryin' to take over? You know what they say, 'the spoils of war go to the victors. Us, me. Not this little fuck. He's gonna come for you too, Johnny Angel."

Johnny was surprised to hear the last part. He paused, wanting Boris to keep talking. "What does that mean, 'he's gonna come for me?'"

"The guy is makin' a move. I feel it. We both been around this business long enough, huh? You can tell when a guy is up to something. I can, that's for sure."

Johnny listened closely. Maybe he had underestimated Little Mike. "Yeah, I get it, but I can't okay what you want. Boris, you're my man. I don't give a shit about Little Mike, but he's a Made guy. I can't whack him. I'd be signing my own death sentence. Look, pal, I don't give a shit how many of those guys you kill, just not Little Mike. Take them all out, and Little Mike can go fuck himself then. Isolate him, but don't kill him. That's better." And with that, Johnny returned to eating his delicious meal.

A few moments of contemplation passed before Boris asked, "What if we got a couple of Apollo's guys and left some dope on the scene? It'll look like a dope deal gone bad with some blacks."

Johnny realized that Boris had been giving this much thought. He needed to discourage him. "Try my way and let's see where that takes us," he answered in between mouthfuls. Johnny looked up and noticed Apollo being seated at the other end of the restaurant. He sent the waiter over to have him join their table. "What's up, pal?" Johnny asked. Apollo walked over and hugged

Johnny and then Boris. "Guys, this is Micki, my future ex-wife."

They all laughed, and Johnny said, "Pleased to meet you." He stuck his hand out, and Micki shook it. "So, what brings you downtown?" Johnny asked.

"We were going out to eat, and Micki said she wanted Italian. This is the only Italian restaurant I come to, so here we are. I didn't even think to call you. I figured you'd be playing cards or something."

"Well, I can't blame you for not calling. With Micki on your arm, who the hell would want to call me? Sit down and join us." They ate and drank for a couple of hours. During the meal, people kept coming over to the table to say hello to Johnny. It was rare for Apollo and Boris to be out without their bodyguards but considering who they were with, neither gave it much thought. Apollo was talking about the new construction that was going on and how he just fired the property manager and was looking for someone. "Do you know anybody?" he asked Johnny.

Micki jumped in and said, "How about my brother Jerome? He needs a job."

"Does he have any experience in property management?" She shook her head. "No, but he's a good worker and quick learner."

"Maybe I can find something else for him—but not that."

"Oh, that would be great. This food is fantastic!" She surprised herself by jumping into the conversation like that. She really did not want anything to do with this, but she had no choice. She might as well make it happen as soon as possible. Micki enjoyed spending time with Apollo and, with each date, found it harder to keep up the façade. Johnny and Boris ordered coffee while Apollo and Micki had cocktails to finish off a wonderful meal.

Johnny looked around the table and said, "Boris, we need to get you back to Brooklyn before you turn into a pumpkin."

"Isn't it an ugly duckling? I thought the coach turned into a pumpkin and the person into an ugly duckling?" Apollo joked.

"Well, you're already an ugly duckling, so next for you is a pumpkin." "Ducks…pumpkins… What are you crazy Americans talking about?" Boris exclaimed while raising his hands up. Everyone laughed. Johnny looked at Apollo and said, "I'm going to play cards. What are you guys up to?"

Apollo shook his head. "We'll probably go to the club, then hopefully Micki will come home with me. She hasn't slept with me yet," he said as he laughed and looked at her.

"Oh my God!" Micki exclaimed. "I can't believe you just said that! How embarrassing!" She playfully covered her face as she felt her cheeks flush.

"Well, all you have to do is sleep with him, and he won't be able to embarrass you like that anymore,"

Johnny said. "You guys know how to make a woman feel right at home, I see." The men all laughed as they left the restaurant. But Micki, caught between a rock and a hard place, wasn't laughing. She could not quite believe the mess she had gotten herself into. And worse, she had no idea how she was going to get out of it.

CHAPTER TWENTY-FOUR

The warehouse for Wang Imports L.T.D., another of Lee's companies, was in the lower part of Manhattan on Mott Street. The inside was in total contradiction to the archaic façade. The contemporary furniture and decorations mixed well with the bricked inside walls. Lee rested his briefcase on the large desk and opened it. He removed the manifest of the ship that docked yesterday and read the contents. Mixed with the one thousand containers of electronics and clothing were one hundred containers of swag merchandise. These boxes would be on the streets of the five major cities in the United States within days. Cheng was away, seeing to the details. These shipments came in about once every six or eight weeks, and it was always a busy time once the ship docked.

Lee buzzed his secretary. "Bring me some tea, please." The pretty twenty-year-old secretary came in a minute later with a cup of hot tea. She was wearing a mini skirt and a tube top. The attire was much more suitable for nightlife than the office, but Lee liked her to dress that way. "Lock the door," he said.

She did as he asked and walked over to him. He lifted the tube top and played with her small, firm breast. He unzipped his fly, and she immediately knelt before him. Lee liked to start his day with a blow job.

J.B. got there a minute after Lee was finished with his secretary. Perfect timing. J.B. placed a suitcase full of money on the table. "This pays for the ship that docked in Naples and for the container we are taking now in Miami. My people are with Cheng right now taking that container, but they tell me there are many more containers left."

Lee smiled. "Is that a question or a statement?"

J.B. smiled also. "The question is, are they all accounted for, or can we have more than one?" "We have people in Houston, NY, Los Angeles, Chicago, and Orlando that are taking containers. Apollo gets three, one for N.Y., one for Detroit, and one for Philly. Do you have different cities besides Miami?" "I can use one for Buffalo and one for Montreal. We took ten containers from the Naples ship. I'd take that many here if you can spare them."

Lee shook his head. "Sorry, no can do for this shipment. I will put you down for ten next time. I will give you two more on this go-round."

"Ah, good, that'll help. I appreciate it." There was a slight pause before he added, "I have something else I wanted to talk with you about. I need a couple of computer geeks, preferably from outside the U.S., where they can operate freely."

Lee looked up at him, curious. "What did you have in mind?"

"I want to rob the banking system."

"You want to rob banks online?"

"No. I want to rob the banking system online." J.B. saw Lee's confusion. "Let me explain. I have the knowledge to get us more money than you could ever imagine. I just don't have the means to get there."

"So, you want to hack into a bank?" Lee asked for further clarity.

J.B. smiled again. "Every bank. When a person makes a loan payment or when one bank deals with another bank, there's always a half of a penny here, a quarter of a penny there in interest. So, in the system, there are fractions of cents floating around. I want to go in and collect them all. Have them sent to an off-shore account. If we can tap into these systems and remove all the fraction of cents, we'd make a ton of money."

Lee was fascinated with what J.B. was describing. "Let me see if I got this right. You're saying that in these banks, there are loan payments where they might have an eighth of a cent…but wouldn't you have to get into each individual's bank account for that?"

"No," J.B. said, equaling Lee's excitement. "It's not just loan payments; it's also saving accounts and every kind of bank transaction! These fractions of a penny are just floating in the system. They aren't on anyone's account. That's the beauty of this deal. No one is going to be missing anything! By the time the banks realize anything has happened, we'll have walked off with billions of dollars!"

"Billions with a 'b' or millions with an 'm'?" Lee leaned forward, eyes growing wide with excitement.

J.B. shook his head. "With a 'b' my friend. We're talking billions of dollars in little denominations, all under a penny. Uncensored, not monitored, and for all intents and purposes, hardly anyone even knows they exist. If we get into all the banks in the world and gather up this loose change, we're talking billions."

"How is this possible?"

"The short explanation is that they cannot add a sixteenth of a cent to the books, so it just floats in the system—out of sight out of mind."

Lee's joy was quickly interrupted with concern. "What happens when they do catch on? Will they trace it right back to our account?"

"Yes and no. We'll have all the money funneled to an off-shore numbered account in the Cayman Islands. Every day we'll move that money to four or five numbered accounts and then disperse the funds to shell companies with numbered accounts. They'll have their hands full trying to break the numbered accounts. The Cayman Island banking laws, as you well know, are not going to cooperate with the Feds here. That's already been proven more than once." J.B.'s smile took over his entire face.

"I agree," Lee said. "Except, they might be inclined to help the banking industry instead of the U.S. Federal Government." As an after-thought, he added, "All in all, I'd have to agree with you. It would be a daunting task." Lee wiped his brow as he contemplated the whole thing.

J.B. smiled again. "Not only would it be daunting, but it would also be futile—and I'm not sure they would want this to get out to the public. No, I think they would tighten up their security and bury the whole story. I doubt they would even be able to put a figure on their loss."

Lee was all smiles too. "And you know where to find these half cents?"

"I know exactly where they are. I just need you to help get me there."

***

Raul Romero, the Dominican boss, sat in one of his stash apartments and watched the video his men had taken of Crazy Lou. They had followed him for the better part of a week. Diaz, Raul's cousin, narrated as he showed him the video.

198

"Last Monday at ten in the morning, he went to the car wash. This morning at ten minutes after ten, he went to the car wash again. We think this is the perfect place to hit him." "Why?" Raul asked. "He's always armed and ready. He's always got others around him who are armed and ready.

"In the carwash, he'll never see us coming with all the soap on the windshield."

"Does he go alone?"

"Both times, he's had some chick with him."

"Are there no other chances before next Monday?

"They are all a lot tougher than the carwash." Raul thought for a moment.

"Okay. Monday, we take Crazy Lou out. Any of his people on the streets that day, we take them down too. On Tuesday, we'll see if whoever is left wants to talk or wants war. Yankee will be back at the end of next week, so we need to do this before then."

"Who do you want to do this?"

Raul did not hesitate. "I don't care who you bring with you, but I want to make sure this is done right. You make sure you're there. We're only going to get one chance at him. There can't be no mistakes." Diaz nodded his head, expecting to hear as much from his cousin. "No problem." And that was all that needed to be said.

***

If Diaz would have followed Crazy Lou one more day, he would have watched him meet with Little Mike. The meeting was at a beer distributor on 2nd Ave in East Harlem. At that meeting, Mike pushed a little harder this time. "So, have you thought about the thing with Yankee?"

Crazy Lou had thought about nothing else since his first meeting with Mike. He was so impressed that he was sitting down, plotting with a real live mafia guy. This was the pinnacle of his gangster life. He didn't want to do anything that would make him lose face with Mike. "I can handle it. Word is Yankee will be back in town any day now."

"No sense in letting him get comfortable. Do you know who Apollo in Harlem is?"

Crazy Lou leaned on a pallet of Sam Adam's summer ale. "Sure, everyone knows Apollo. He's king man there."

"I need you to make him a dead king, just like Yankee. Can you handle that?"

Louis hesitated. "I can, but I'd have to check out his routine. I don't know anything about him."

"Okay, as long as you can handle it. I'd rather not use my own guys. This way, they won't know it's coming from me. We'll worry about Apollo after we take care of Yankee."

"Once we hit Yankee, the shit's gonna hit the fan. Those Colombians will be coming out of the woodwork like fucking cockroaches, man. We're gonna have a real war on our hands."

Mike waved his hand as if to say, 'no big deal. "Just step on them like you do a cockroach. I'll supply you with some men if you need help." Mike had no intention of doing anything for Crazy Lou. He just wanted him to be comfortable. His only concern was destroying Johnny Angel.

CHAPTER TWENTY-FIVE

Malaga, in Southern Spain, is one of the oldest cities in the world. It lies on the Costa del Sol of the Mediterranean Sea, about sixty-two miles east of the Strait of Gibraltar and eighty miles north of Africa. It is the southernmost city in Europe. The warm climate and ocean make it a big vacation and tourist spot each year. Malaga is a money town. The streets are filled with expensive Italian automobiles, and million-dollar yachts are docked one after another. Ivan sat at an open-air gelato shop, watching a yacht a block away. The last of the Solnstevskaya Bratva's crew was there on that yacht. The two men on board had been hiding there since last week. Ivan had systematically taken out the entire crew Mika had left behind.

There were fourteen of them to start with when he came back from America, and now the last two were in his sights. The area was too crowded with tourists to make a move here. He had to be patient. Boris would not be pleased if they set off an international incident. He watched as the two men came on deck from below. Standing there, they looked around for a moment and started to disembark. They got into a new Maserati that was parked in front of the yacht.

Ivan picked up his walkie-talkie and spoke. "Mama and Papa Bear on the way to Grandma's house."

A man who was sitting and waiting on a motorcycle replied into his headpiece, "Got them, instruct, please."

"Backup is two minutes behind you. Then deliver the package."

"Okay," Ivan spoke again into the walkie-talkie. "Number two, where are you?"

Two men in a silver Porsche answered the call. They were "Coming upon them now, sir. I see them ahead." The motorcyclist saw the Porsche coming up fast behind the target's vehicle. He accelerated and went to pass the Maserati. As he came alongside the driver's window, he pulled out a pistol and took aim. Inside the Maserati, the two men were intent on getting to their destination. They had finally agreed that they would no longer win this war. They decided that it would be best if they left the comforts of the yacht and disappear. They were headed for Estonia, where their Bratva was strong. The driver had noticed the motorcycle behind him since they left the docks. He watched as it pulled up next to him and saw the pistol barely a blink of a second before the man fired.

The driver nailed the Maserati, and the powerful 405 HP V-8 engine roared to life as the back passenger window blew out from the bullet. The motorcycle could not keep up with the Maserati, but the Porsche was right behind it. The passenger in the Porsche leaned out the window with an automatic rifle and opened fire. The back windshield exploded as three bullets ripped into the driver. The Maserati swerved and spun out of control. It went off the highway at one hundred miles an hour and flipped in the air. In spectacular fashion, it went crashing off the road, tumbling down the roadside, finally exploding into a ball of fire. The Porsche and the motorcycle drove off and reported back to Ivan. "Big Bad Wolf ate Mama and Papa bear."

***

Crazy Lou shoved the clip into the pistol and sent a round into the chamber. He did not bother to put the safety on. People were stupid to carry guns with the safety on; they'd never be able to use them quickly in a jam. He prided himself on always being ready. Nobody was going to get the drop on him, that's for sure. He walked into his kitchen and poured himself a cup of coffee. He thought about what was going to happen. As soon as Yankee got back in town, Louis had a surprise for him. Then he would take Raul out too.

In one day, he would eliminate both of his rivals and take over. He was close now with the Italians, and that was sweet. Yeah, the Colombians would come, but he would be ready for them too. This was his turf, and he was confident he could defend it. Grandiose dreams danced in his head as he took a long sip of a fresh cafe. He laid out a couple of lines to start the day. Ah, a great pick-me-up. He called Carmen, his little sex doll, and told her to be ready in ten minutes. Louis would run through the car wash this morning while Carmen was giving him head. It always excited him to have sex in public like that. No one could actually see them, but just the thought that there were people all around aroused him.

He grabbed a brown paper bag from the kitchen counter and opened it. Holding the pistol in his right hand, he put his hand in the bag. If there was a sneak attack while he walked to his car, he would fire just as quickly as his attackers. Always ready, he reminded himself, always ready. When he got to his car, he walked around it to make sure there were no dings or dents. He loved his '67 Impala. Once he caught some kids leaning on it, and he beat the shit out of two of them. Everyone on the block knew better than to go near Crazy Lou's car. It was a classic, in mint condition. Louis got in and drove the two blocks to where Carmen was waiting outside for him. She jumped in, and they drove off. The carwash was on the next block, so when he was done, Carmen could just walk back. He had no time to drive her home. The brushless wash had two cars ahead of him this morning. As he pulled in line, he put on a Marc Anthony CD and cranked it up.

The first car waiting pulled into the wash. The back garage door closed as the wash started up. After a few minutes, the garage door opened to allow the next car in line to enter the wash. Louis was next. When the big door finally opened, Louis tapped in the carwash code on the pad. The big machine started blinking, and the Pull Forward sign lit up. Louis pulled up, threw the car in neutral, unzipped his pants, and took out his vial of coke from his shirt pocket. Carmen immediately went down on him as he snorted a few lines off the back of his hand. The wash started up and passed over the Impala twice with a hard rinse. The third pass was all soap, and as it covered the windshield, Louis was about to bust a nut. He never saw the two men dressed in yellow rain gear approach from the front of the car. They opened fire, and when the windshield exploded, Crazy Lou's shocked face was painfully visible. He had no time to react as four bullets ripped through his body. Crazy Lou died with a mask of ecstasy planted on his face and his hand reaching for the brown paper bag. 'Always ready' Lou was just not ready today. Carmen, faithful to the end, laid in his lap, Crazy Lou's cock still in the mouth of her lifeless body. Blood was everywhere, the carwash pads still whirring, soapsuds covering the car. The two men in the yellow rain suits quickly exited the carwash before anyone really knew what had happened.

Johnny had been spending his time between Sing and Theresa. Theresa was a hot-blooded Puerto Rican, and the sex was fantastic. She had a great body, silky skin, and was soft in all the right places. She was also the mother of his daughter, so he considered her his main woman. Sing was thinner yet just as beautiful and sexy. Her skin was paler than Theresa's olive complexion but just as soft and silky. She was not as experienced a lover as Theresa, but what she lacked in experience, she made up for in her desire to please him. He had the best of both worlds and was caught up in the lust of it all.

He had five years to make up for. Tonight, he would take a break and not see either of them. He was having dinner with Yankee, who had just returned from Colombia. When Johnny entered the Polo Grounds, he immediately noticed the extra security. Everyone relaxed when they saw it was Johnny. He made his way to the office, where Yankee came around the desk to greet him. "What's with all the extra men?"

Yankee smiled. "Raul whacked Crazy Lou and four of his top men." He shrugged his shoulders like he was indifferent to the whole thing. "Everyone's just a little over-cautious right now."

"You damn Latinos are too hot-blooded," Johnny replied jokingly.

"Yeah, well, it's more peaceful without him. I can assure you of that."

"I think we should eat somewhere else tonight," Johnny suggested. Yankee agreed. They drove up to Westchester County and ate at a nice Italian restaurant in Hastings-on-the-Hudson. Johnny and Yankee ate at one table, and Yankee's bodyguards ate at the next table. The bodyguards took turns eating; one guy watched the door while another had a fork in his mouth.

"So, how was your trip?" Johnny asked between forkfuls of food. Yankee nodded his head.

"It was good. I hooked J.B. up with everything he wanted. That should bring in a lot of cash. I have to deal with the problem in Mexico. They act like it's the Wild West down there. I'm putting together a meeting with the top three cartels there. They have to stop all this violence and killings."

"Why? Are you getting bad press? Is it hurting business?" Johnny took a break and took a sip of vino.

"They have gotten too big and way too stupid. I'm sending Tito down there tomorrow. If he can't fix things, we'll cut them off and send in a few hit squads to clean up. It's that serious."

"I might need a team to take care of some of Boris's mess in Brooklyn. I'll let you know as it unfolds." Johnny said.

"No problem. I got good guys I can send. Those fucking Russians are like the Mexicans, yes?"

"Not quite as bad, but close. You gotta love Boris, though. He wants to kill everybody." Both men laughed, thinking about their Russian friend.

Over the years, Johnny had used all four of his ethnic groups to do work for one another. It always helped cover the real trail. Sending Asians to kill Colombians or Russians to kill blacks always had the other side confused—and kept law enforcement in the dark also. With that kind of power behind him, Johnny Angel was the most deadly and feared gangster in town. Everyone knew that Johnny wielded great power, and he could use it as he chose when he chose.

CHAPTER TWENTY-SIX

The Pleasant Avenue regime of the Genovese Family, commonly known as the Harlem crew, had been meeting on Tuesday mornings for more than thirty years. The only thing different today was that no soldier could take any longer approach and speak with his caporegime.

Since Johnny had taken over as captain of the crew, he invoked this law, and many were unhappy about it. They felt slighted, like he thought he was above them. Many silently wanted Johnny gone because of the disrespect they felt, though they would never show their displeasure. The others were loyal. This split in the ranks fed a growing sense of tension. The boss and the underboss were both under indictment. The boss was already sitting in jail with no bail, and yesterday, the underboss's bail had been revoked. With the two leaders of the Family behind bars, there was more uncertainty in the family. There were eighteen regimes, and now a five-captain panel became the ruling members to lead the Family. Johnny was one of them.

Johnny knew that this new role would bring more heat from the F.B.I. As he walked into the social club that Tuesday morning, he wanted to distance himself even further from the soldiers. He stopped and hugged each of the soldiers and asked how they were doing. That was a mere show of respect because they already had been ordered by Danny not to talk about any business with their captain. Mario Lorenza was one of the unhappy ones. He was mad from the start, believing he should have been promoted to captain when Ralphie Arms died. Not only was he passed over, but now this ungrateful bastard Johnny Angel was refusing to talk to anyone!

He'd be damned if he was going to take this lying down. Mario was in his mid-sixties and had been a made man for forty years, making tons of money for the Family. He was a good earner and had done plenty of work. He had been silently recruiting members to see where he stood. The way he figured it, he had half the crew, and the other half would stay on Johnny's side. The last member that he was not sure about was Sully. He and Sully had been friends for many years, but Sully was close to Ralphie— and Ralphie was the one that wanted Johnny to succeed him. It was time to see where Sully stood. Mario walked over to where Sully was standing.

"What's up, pal?" Sully looked over and smiled.

"Hey Mario, how are you?"

"Good, good." Mario looked over at Johnny, saying hello to everyone. "What do you think about that?" he asked, nodding his head in Johnny's direction.

"About what?"

"Can't talk to our skipper."

211

"I think it's smart. Makes a lot of sense."

"I think it's disrespectful. It's like insinuating that we're rats and can't be trusted." He scowled.

Sully laughed good and hard over that. "Mario, we can't be trusted," he said and walked away. Mario crossed Sully off his side of the list. When Danny came in, he too said hello to everyone, and when he got to Mario, he hugged him.

Mario said, "Danny, I need to speak with Johnny." Danny shook his head.

"What's up?"

"What, do I need an interpreter to speak with my skipper? I got important business."

"I'm your interpreter, Mario. Tell me what the problem is."

"I don't like this, Danny. I'm offended that I can't speak with my capo."

"You can speak with him, Mario. It just needs to go through me." He needed to be careful here. Being upset was one thing—but suggesting rebellion would be quite something different. He decided to bite his tongue, for now anyway.

"I need to scab a job I'm gonna do down on Hester Street," he quickly added, not wanting to press his hand too much. "What union?"

"All the unions. I wanna scab the whole job. I'm gonna gut this six-story building and remodel it. I wanna scab the whole job."

Danny nodded his head. "Okay," was all he said and walked off. Mario shook his head. These guys have got to be kidding me. I remember when they were just street punks, he thought to himself. It was time to feel out the other captains on the ruling panel. He knew he could count on at least three of them. After that, he'd have to work on the remaining two. If Johnny just disappeared, it was more than likely they would make him act captain. That was a start. He could live with that.

After Danny made the rounds, he and Johnny went outside to talk. Johnny would leave when the talk was over, and Danny would wait to go back inside until after Johnny was gone. Then, in case someone asked for him, Danny would say he's gone already.

"So, what's important?" Johnny asked.

Danny shook his head. "I'm getting bad vibes from Mario. He kept pressing to see you. He said he was offended by your new rules. You think he might be wired up?"

Johnny thought for a second. "No, he wouldn't complain that he was offended if he was wired. Think about it. He'd want to get close to show his love, all that bullshit. What does he want?"

"Wants to scab a job on Hester Street. I don't see what's so pressing to talk to you about that for."

"I think he's got a resentment. He thinks he should've gotten skipper, not me."

"Maybe you should have a talk with him and let him know this is the way you want to operate and that you mean no disrespect. Then, get him to relax and loosen up a little."

Johnny stopped walking, faced Danny, and said, "No. Fuck him and the horse he rode in on. I'm skipper, and it's too bad if he doesn't like it. I ain't explaining nothing to him. He'll do what I tell him to do."

"Okay, it's your call."

"What else you got?"

"Nothing of any importance. I can handle the rest."

"Good," Johnny replied. "Now for some good news. The boss said the troops needed to pay for his defense. So everyone needs to kick an envelope up. Make sure everybody brings one next Tuesday. If there's nothing else, I'm outta here. See you later."

"What about Mario's scab job?" Johnny laughed.

"Tell him he has my blessing, and I said to add five percent on top for me.

That'll really piss him off." He smiled. "I don't get it. What gives? You know that's gonna make him crazy. Why throw gas on the fire?"

"After all these years we been together, you ain't learned shit, have you? Obviously, Mario is resentful. It's better to have him openly mad than silently plotting while he's acting like he's my best friend. He's mad, so if I make him even madder, he'll show his hand more sooner than later like this."

Danny shook his head. "Yeah, I guess that's why you're the skipper."

"Yeah, and don't you forget that," Johnny said, laughing again as he walked away.

***

"What are you crying about?" Apollo asked, lying in bed, having just made love to Micki. It was even better than he had anticipated, but he couldn't understand her crying.

She shook her head and raised her shoulders. "I don't know. I just always find a way to mess up in relationships," she said as she covered her face with her hands.

Apollo laughed. "Come here, girl." She inched closer to him and lay with her head on his chest. "I'm the one who usually messes up the relationship. Maybe two screw-ups like us can make it work?" Apollo said, trying to get her to lighten up.

She smiled, but she was full of guilt. She didn't want to do this, but the F.B.I. forced her. At this point, she was ready to face the consequences and do her time, but she couldn't risk getting Grandma in trouble. So she was stuck between two horrible places. Then, she realized she was crying again.

"Hey. I got good news," Apollo said, getting her in a better mood. "I've got some work for your brother." She wiped her eyes and sat up.

"Really? Doing what?"

"What, are you his manager now? If he's willing to start off small at the bottom, we can always use a good man."

"Yeah, he'll do anything. Jobs are hard to find these days."

"Tell him to be at the club tonight, nine o'clock. Black suit, black shirt, black tie. Make sure he has proper I.D. and social security number. Tell him to see Donald. He's the owner, he'll hook him up."

"Oh, I thought you were the owner?"

Apollo made a face and said, "Now what makes you say that?"

She quickly covered up by saying, "All the girls at the club say you're the real owner."

"Well, don't listen to gossip. No, I'm just a customer." Apollo's natural defenses jumped in. This was the first time Micki brought up any business. He thought it was innocent enough and didn't pay any more attention to it. "I'm gonna take a shower; then I got some things to do. I'll see you tonight?" He flung the covers off of him and sat up, swinging his legs over the side of the bed.

"I hope so. I'm off tonight," she said, smiling and calming herself down as best she could under the circumstances.

"Good." He pushed himself off the bed and went to the shower. She immediately called Jerome. Maybe this would be enough for them to leave her alone now that she opened the door for Jerome.

CHAPTER TWENTY-SEVEN

Mario was in a good mood as he bit into his pear. It was juicy and sweet. It wasn't too hard or too soft; it was just perfect. He reflected on his decision about Johnny Angel. He had to go, but he could not risk seeking a sanction on this from the ruling panel. He had to go it alone. He'd deal with the consequences after the fact. If he were careful, no one would ever find out he had anything to do with it.

These younger members were ruining everything. They were all too selfish and weak. They worried only about their little world. The secret society they swore allegiance to was all lip service. When push came to shove, they flipped. And they wanted to run as much as they could get away with, but they only acted as a man of honor until the law stepped in. Once the law grabbed them, they had no benefit. Mario would not sit by and become flunky to that kind of disrespect, that kind of bullshit. To add insult to injury, Johnny demanded five percent of his score on the construction deal. What balls he had! Mario had a few guys under him, and he promised that he would propose them to be straightened out if they did this. Once the job was over, he would kill two of them. The third guy, Anthony "TD" Donotta, had been with him for years. Mario might need him in the future so that he would be spared.

The restaurant they were in served breakfast, and when the waitress walked away, they talked in hushed whispers. The Conte brothers, Joey and Guy, nodded their heads as Mario spoke about the importance of having Johnny disappear.

TD asked, "Where we gonna take the body?"

"Upstate," Mario replied. "Go up the day before and dig a hole, a deep hole, then we just dump him in there after we're done. In fact, you two," he said, pointing to the brothers, "will go dig the hole. Only you two will ever know where this arrogant piece of shit is buried at." They nodded their consent. They were ready for this piece of work, knowing Mario had opened a door they had been waiting for. "Make sure the hole is deep enough that animals don't dig him up to eat. The least we can do is give him a decent resting place." Mario laughed at that, and the others joined in. As an after-thought, he added, "Better make that hole big enough for two just in case his errand-boy Danny gets in the way." They spent the next hour going over the best place to grab Johnny, how to whack him and how to take him up to the burial site.

"Don't underestimate Johnny Angel. He didn't get to where he's at today by being stupid," Mario said. He then warned, "They ain't stupid. And if we fuck up, we're all dead." "Next Tuesday, when we all meet, you follow Johnny from there. Spend as much time as you need to make this go smoothly. When you think you got his schedule down pat, we'll meet to work out the final details. TD, remember this—if Johnny sees you guys following him, he'll kill you very quickly and very painfully."

"So you've said," replied TD. "I ain't worried about it."

Mario made a face. "Well, I am, so humor me and be extra careful." When the Conte brothers left, Mario turned to TD. "When this is done, you go with them to bury Johnny. Just tell them you wanna make sure it's done right. When you get there, leave them all in the hole, the brothers and Johnny."

TD nodded his head. He didn't like these orders, but this is the life they lived.

* * *

"Fuck!" Little Mike slammed his hand down on the table. "What the hell happened there?"

Chilly shook his head. "Don't know. All I know is that they ambushed him in the carwash. He was getting a blowjob while his car was going through the wash. Two guys with rain gear and automatic weapons walked into the wash and opened fire. They killed the girl too. Word is it was the Dominicans. They hit four others from Louie's crew too."

"So, where do they stand now?"

Chilly made a left turn and glanced over to Little Mike. He shook his head again. "They're finished. What's left of them called for a sit-down, and Yankee put an end to the war. They've been down-sized to only two blocks in Washington Heights. Now the Dominicans got the rest of it sewed up."

Mike was red in the face. "Motherfucker, this Johnny Angel keeps getting lucky. I'm starting to think he really does have an angel watching out for his ass. Okay, what about that spook up in Harlem. Any headway there?" "Still trying to find an in with them. Nothing yet."

"You got any good fucking news, or are you just full of negative shit?" Mike was getting madder by the minute.

Chilly hated having all bad news, but he wouldn't start making shit up that would get him killed. "I can start clocking this Apollo and do him myself if you want." He shrugged his shoulders. Mike thought that was a good idea, but he couldn't risk Chilly getting caught up in this mess; that would come right back to him. No, this had to be done on the sneak. They needed to regroup and figure things out. Mike was sure of one thing—and that was Johnny Angel needed to go. He had more work to do on the when and how.

***

Theresa brought the men espresso and pastries and left them alone. She and Angel went into the bedroom so the men could have their privacy. Johnny poured a shot of Sambuca for Yankee and then one for himself. "So, how's the Mexico thing going?"

Yankee nodded. "Yeah, I'm sending Tito back again tomorrow. We'll see what happens. How's everything with you? You back in the groove yet?"

Johnny laughed. "It's like riding a bike. You just jump right back on and pedal away."

"What, like you took time off? You made more money the last five years in the joint than most people make in a lifetime." Yankee said smilingly. They clinked their glasses. "Salute," they said to each other and downed the sweet-tasting liqueur.

Johnny loved the slight burning sensation of Sambuca. Every once in a while, he could get his hands on a bottle in the joint. To have a glass now, whenever he wanted it...that was sweet. That was the taste of freedom.

"What do you stay in for? You got more money than God. Shit, if I had your money, I'd throw mine away," said Johnny.

Yankee laughed. "I'm like you, my friend. First off, I'm a gangster right down to my bones. Secondly, I couldn't leave if I wanted to; our cartel is like your Mafioso; we don't offer a retirement package. No gold watches and pats on the back. Besides, where the fuck would I go?"

It was Johnny's turn to laugh. "Oh, don't kid yourself. We have a retirement package. You just wouldn't like the benefits."

Angel and Theresa came into the room. "She wants to say goodnight," Theresa said. Angel jumped up onto Johnny's lap. She put her arms around him and squeezed tight. "Goodnight, Daddy."

Johnny hugged her back. "Wow, that was a great hug," he said with a big smile. "Now, give me a kiss." The little girl kissed his cheek and then ran to Yankee. She gave him the same big hug and kiss. "Goodnight, Uncle Hector."

"Ah, goodnight, my little angel," he said, staring proudly at her. Theresa stood there waving her hand, "Come now, sweetheart." When she left the room, Johnny said, "That kid is too smart. She's something else."

"Yes," Yankee agreed. "She truly is an angel."

Johnny poured another shot of Sambuca for the two of them. "Salute,'" he said, tapping Yankee's glass. And before another moment passed, he added, "I need you to go see Boris."

Yankee downed his shot and made a face as the liqueur burned its way to his stomach. "And?"

"It's a little delicate," replied Johnny. "I think he's planning to whack Little Mike, who's a made guy. Different family but still the same problem. I told him 'no' he couldn't do it. I even gave him the okay to whack everybody involved except for Mike."

"But you don't think he's going to listen... So, you want me to talk him out of it?"

"The problem is if it comes back that it was Boris, and I'm sure it will, then they'll make me whack him. I won't have a choice. He needs to do this my way."

"I'll go see him. What doesn't he understand about that?"

"Yank, we're talking about the crazy Russian Boris. We love him, but he's fucking nuts, you know that." Another round poured, and the glasses clinked once more.

CHAPTER TWENTY-EIGHT

The office looked neat and orderly. It was small but cozy. Donald liked to have the young girls prance around half-naked while they set up for opening each night. Micki's brother Jerome took the whole scene in as he tapped on the door. "You got a minute, boss?"

"What do you need?" Donald asked.

Jerome bounced from foot to foot and said, "I got a friend that has three sixty-inch plasma televisions. He wants two hundred apiece."

"What brand are they?"

"Sony, I think. If you take all three, I can probably get 'em for five hundred bucks."

"That's a great deal. How hot are they?" Jerome smiled. This would be the first infraction in his case—buying and possessing stolen property.

"It just fell off the back of the truck."

Donald was excited. He loved getting a deal on something, and this was too good to be true. "I'll take all three of them."

"Great. I get ten percent from you. That's fifty bucks."

"What the fuck is that for? You are shaking me down?"

"No. Come on, boss man, it's still a good deal for you. I need to make something." He shrugged his shoulders innocently.

"Why didn't you just say five-fifty then?"

"I wanted to be honest with you. That's still a great deal. I make fifty bucks, and we're all happy. You can pay me in blow if you want."

Donald's eyes grew wide. "Blow! What makes you think I've got blow?"

"Whoa, take it easy. I'm just saying."

"I know what you're just saying, and I don't like the implication." Jerome threw his hands up.

"Okay, boss, no problem. Cash works for me too."

Donald laughed. "Just fucking with you. Bring the T.V.'s, and I'll have some kick-ass blow for you." He gave him a wink. Jerome was all smiles now. His case was moving into high gear. He'd have something on Donald, and hopefully, they could flip him to set up Apollo and then work Apollo to get Johnny Angel. He took out his cell phone and said, "I'll have them delivered right now."

***

"Raise," Johnny said and threw two hundred on the table.

"Two hundred dollar raise," said the houseman who added Johnny's two hundred to the pot. He said, "Two more to you, " to the next player."

Danny and Nick walked in and watched for a minute. Danny came over to Johnny and bent down to whisper to him. "We have to talk." Johnny did not answer. All the other players except one went out. He called the two hundred dollar raise.

Johnny dropped his cards on the table. "Three fours," he said. The other man threw his cards face down on the table. "You win," he said.

"What do you got?" Johnny asked.

"Doesn't matter. You win," the man replied and went to throw his cards in the dead pile.

"It does matter," Johnny said. "I paid to see your cards, and I want to see them," he said, tapping his index finger on the table.

"And I don't want to show them, so now what?" he said with an attitude. He did not know who Johnny was, but he was about to find out.

"So now you either flip your cards over, or I flip you over." Johnny smiled at him. The houseman knew trouble was coming, so he jumped right in. "I'm sorry, sir, but you have to show your cards if the bet was called." The man looked at the house guy like he was crazy.

"The bet wasn't called. I called his bet."

"Same difference, sir. That's house rules." By this time, Danny and Nick were standing behind the man.

"Well, fuck house rules. That's stupid," the man said as he leaned back and crossed his arms over his chest. Johnny looked at Danny and nodded his head. Danny pulled the guy up by his neck with his arm wrapped around it. Nick moved quickly and hammered a couple of blows to the man's stomach. Johnny got up and walked slowly over to that end of the table. Nick and Danny had hold of the man's arms, one on either side. Johnny walked up to him.

"Are you having a bad day? Are you losing tonight? This is your chance to apologize." He smiled again, mere inches from his face. The man looked at Johnny. The fear in his eyes was apparent.

"I'm sorry, that was stupid of me."

Johnny nodded his head. It was not good to embarrass a man in front of others. You'd have an enemy for life. If you weren't going to kill him, you'd have to leave him with some dignity. "Let him go," he said. They released him. Johnny held out his hand. "My name is Johnny."

The man looked at Johnny like he thought he was being fucked with. He shook Johnny's hand. "Marty," he said.

"Okay, Marty, now do you understand the house rules? If you don't want your cards shown, you don't call?"

He nodded.

"Good, then let's play cards." Johnny turned to the poker table and said, "Deal me out a few hands and watch my money." Johnny looked back at Nick and Danny and nodded toward the front door. When they were outside, they walked down the sidewalk.

"You're getting soft in your old age," Danny said. "Was a time not so long ago where we would have put that fool in the hospital."

"I didn't wanna ruin the game. Besides, he didn't know who I was."

"Obviously." Nicky laughed.

"What's up?" Johnny asked.

Danny pointed to Nicky, who spoke up. "I think we found Uncle Lenny."

"Really? Where's he at?"

"Well, that call he made to you came from Little Rock, Arkansas."

"Damn! What the hell is he doing there?"

"Hiding out," Danny said.

"No shit, you think so?" Johnny asked sarcastically. "When I get home, I'll check some maps and come up with a plan. Have Charlie, Joe, and Gino on standby."

"Which Joe?" Danny asked.

"Joey Bats. I'll meet with you in the morning. Good job, Nicky." Johnny turned around, walked back to the door, and headed inside the poker game. He would deal with Uncle Lenny tomorrow. Tonight, he wanted to enjoy the game.

He patted Marty on the back and took his seat. He rifled through his money and playfully punched old man Roy sitting next to him. "You took a hundred. Give it back."

***

Lee sat back on the plush Italian leather sofa. He rubbed his hand over the soft seat cushion, obviously the finest quality leather. "Everything is set up in China for you. Just tell me what they need to do."

"I'd like to go there myself if possible," JB replied.

"No problem. I will send Cheng with you to make things easier. I trust you have all the bank accounts ready to go?"

"Yes, there are three in the Cayman Islands and two in Switzerland. The money will go through ten different bank accounts and then be transferred to the Cayman and Swiss accounts. From there, they'll be sent to where you and I have accounts set up for ourselves."

"How long do you think the whole process will take?" "As soon as we're up and running, we can start getting the money. I'd like to have a two-week run. In that span of time, I think we can cash out hundreds of millions."

Lee made a face. "Do you think they will catch on so quickly?"

"That's the tricky part. There's no way of telling. This may go undetected for years. We're going after Chase Bank and Bank of America. They're so big it's our best shot to have a long run. They may never realize there has been a breach in their system, especially because we're taking money that they don't even know exists."

Lee laughed. "I think they will somehow figure they've been breached but not realize what we have done."

"That's a real possibility, but once they know there has been a breach, they will fix it, and the gig is up, but the damage will have been done." "When do you want to go to China?"

"I'm ready," JB said.

Lee nodded his head. "I will arrange it. We need an account for Johnny also."

"Johnny gets twenty percent of my cut for hooking us up," JB stated.

"And he will get the same from my end," Lee replied.

CHAPTER TWENTY-NINE

Johnny cut his French toast and bit in. He looked over at Danny, who was pushing eggs around his plate. "What's the matter with you? You look like shit," he said as he shoved another piece of French toast in his mouth.

"Look like shit? It's fucking nine o'clock Saturday morning. I didn't get home till five, but I can't sleep late… Why? Because you wanna meet at nine o'clock in the fucking morning." Danny was clearly irritated. He averted his eyes from Johnny.

"Oh, you want some cheese to go with that wine or what?" Johnny shook his head. "I played cards until three, went home, researched everything, came up with a master plan, and here, I am bright-eyed and bushy-tailed. I swear you're getting old and useless."

"Yeah, good for you. Let's hear your master plan."

"Well, my master plan changed because I remembered something very important. Do you remember Linda Milano?"

Danny shrugged. "Sure. She was my first blow job. How can I forget her." "You blew her?" Johnny asked, laughing at his own joke.

Danny's bad mood lightened, and he laughed too. "I see you're not just bright-eyed and bushy-tailed— you're a fucking comedian."

Johnny was still laughing. "Okay," he said, getting serious again. "Before I went to the joint, I saw her one day while she was here visiting. She married some Army or Air Force guy. Anyway, guess where she lives?" Danny shook his head, and the mood returned. "Johnny, I'm in no mood to play twenty questions. I got a hangover that's killing me."

"You really are turning into a little bitch. She lives in Little Rock, Arkansas. Hello! Little Rock, Arkansas. Linda Milano. Little Rock, Arkansas. Uncle Lenny." Johnny had a big smile on his face.

Danny just looked at him. "So what, are you gonna get Linda Milano to whack Uncle Lenny?"

"Obviously, you don't see the beauty in all this. How are we gonna find Lenny if we go there? Wait around all the Italian restaurants 'til he shows up? Linda's there already. Look, she's from the neighborhood. She used to hang with us. We can trust her. You have Gino call her. Tell her Uncle Lenny stole a bunch of money, and we need to find him. We think he's out there somewhere. Let her start checking around. In the meantime, we'll start doing research from here. Check new phone accounts, new electric, gas, HBO accounts, etc. You get it?"

"Ain't it dangerous letting her know we want Lenny and then him turning up dead?"

"He ain't gonna turn up dead, he ain't gonna turn up at all. He needs to disappear for good. Then I'll see our friends and tell them Lenny isn't showing up in any court. Linda knows her way around; she can be helpful. We'll drop some good money in her lap, and she'll be fine."

"I like the whole searching plan, but I ain't crazy about contacting Linda. I'm not sure if that's a good move." Danny popped his knuckles as he thought about the proposal.

Johnny nodded his head. "Okay, you run it your way. You're in charge. Just find Lenny."

"Oh, thanks."

"You're welcome," Johnny replied with a big smile. "And don't take all damn year about it either."

***

Russian Paul had four bodyguards. He wasn't taking any chances trusting Boris to keep the peace. He just finished a long meeting with his entire Bratva. Since Vladimir had been assassinated, the brotherhood had lost business and lots of money. Boris had even managed to take control of their lucrative prostitution business in Spain. That took a lot of money out of their hands, and now Little Mike was getting twenty-five percent of whatever they had left. At the meeting, he implemented some changes that should start fresh cash flowing in. No doubt the Bratva was weakened, but it was still a strong money earner.

Paul needed to go by and see his young sweetheart. He was infatuated with her and had to go by at least once a day, usually around two in the afternoon. She was thirty years his junior and quite unlike his out-of-shape wife. Her name was Olga, and she had a strong, tight body. He phoned her to let her know he was on the way to her apartment. Following his orders, she would unlock the door and get into bed naked with a toy. She should be worked into a frenzy by the time he got there. That was how they always had their meetings. That really turned Russian Paul on.

When they pulled in front of her building, the driver stayed with the car, and the other three bodyguards got out with Paul. They walked up the steps to Olga's third-floor apartment. One bodyguard stayed in the hallway outside the apartment door. The other two entered the apartment with Paul. Olga was a beautiful twenty-one-year-old illegal alien from Poland. She hated Paul but was stuck with him and his fat sweaty body that repulsed her.

When she was approached by Boris and his men the other day, she was delighted by their offer. Boris had given her a thousand dollars and promised her a Social

Security number and a U.S. passport plus four thousand more dollars if she would let them know when Paul was coming again.

After Paul called her, she made a call to Boris, eager to get her reward. When Paul walked into the apartment with his two bodyguards, they were completely taken by surprise when four men got the jump on them. All three men were ordered to their knees. Stephan Elson was in charge of the hit team, so he stepped forward and put the silenced pistol to Paul's head. He simply said, "Call your buddy in from the hallway," in a quiet tone. Stephan nodded to Dex, who cracked the apartment door open. Paul said, "Peter, come in, please." As soon as the bodyguard stepped into the apartment, he had a silenced pistol to his temple.

"On your knees," Dex ordered. Stephan, Dex, and Boris' other men stood beside the four kneeling men. Paul made the sign of the cross as they were all executed. Stephan walked into the bedroom, where Olga was waiting for her reward. She smiled at Stephan, and he thought about having sex with her before he killed her. Unfortunately, there was no time for that. "Thanks for all your help," he said and proceeded to shoot her once in the head. She fell over, betrayed, bloodied, and dead. The four killers walked down the three flights of steps.

Stephan walked over to the parked car. "Keep your hands on the steering wheel," he said to the driver as he pointed a gun at the man. "Do you know who I am?" Stephan Elson and his father were the two most notorious killers in the Russian Mafia underworld. The driver nodded his head. "Good, now listen carefully, and you will live today, unlike your four comrades who were not so fortunate. What is your name?"

"Alex," replied the frightened driver. "Okay, Alex. I want you to gather your entire Bratva and tell them that Boris is the new boss and you are now all working for us. The next time one of you makes a deal with the Italians, we will kill all of you. You will bring us twenty-five percent of all your earnings each week. You understand?"

The driver nodded his head, not trusting his voice.

"Good. Here is my number. Call me when you have your meeting, and we will attend to settle this once and for all. You either join us or die. Now you may go."

When Stephan got back to Boris's place, Ivan and Maxim were there. Stephan relayed everything that had happened and the message he sent to the driver. Boris laughed.

"How many of them do you figure are left?"

"Under twenty," Maxim said, "it is easy to recruit more."

"And if the Italians join in, there are many more," Ivan added. "I'm hoping that is the case. Then Johnny will have no choice about Little Mike dying. Let's wait 'til they call Stephan and see where we are."

Stephan said, "I have an idea if you'd like to hear it."

Boris smiled. "By all means, what is it?"

"When they call me for the meeting, I should go there and kill them all. This way, they have no more connection to the Italians. We take over everything. We get one hundred percent instead of twenty-five."

"I love it." Boris laughed.

"Hold on," Ivan said. "The problem is we don't know what we're taking over. We have no idea what business they have, so we won't know what to take over."

"But it's a brilliant idea," Boris chimed in. "We can work with them until we get to know what business they have and then kill them all." All four men laughed at the thought. "Nice country America," Boris said in delight.

***

"Hey boss, you got a minute?"

"Sure," Donald said. "What's up?"

239

"My friends really liked that coke you gave me for the T.V. They want to know if you can get them a little weight."

Donald was glad to make a few bucks on the side. "I don't want to meet anyone," he said sternly. "As long as you handle it, we can do something."

Jerome smiled. "I can do that, but don't forget to take care of me."

Donald shook his head. "There you go shaking me down again. I'll leave you room to tack something on for yourself, but my price comes to me untouched. The least you can do is take a taste from their side, not mine."

"Fair enough, boss." Jerome was pleased with the way he moved right into the action. Building this case was turning out to be easier than any of them had imagined. "If you can have a quarter of a key tonight, that would be good." "No problem," Donald responded. "No problem at all. I'll give it to you for sixty-five hundred. You charge them seventy-five. You make a dime on the deal. Don't get greedy and go too high, or you'll blow the deal."

"Great! Thanks, boss." Jerome was all smiles. He wanted to tell him that no price would blow this deal. Instead, he just smiled at what he knew was coming.

CHAPTER THIRTY

It had been a long time since Boris had been to this part of Manhattan. The neighborhood seemed unchanged, unlike Brighton Beach, which looked more like Russia than America. He looked around as he entered the Polo Grounds Lounge. His bodyguards sat at the first table. Boris did not need them there at Yankee's place, but he needed them everywhere else his travels took him. He got to the last table when he was stopped by the same man who stopped Johnny the first night he went there. Boris said, "Tell Yankee Boris is here."

This time, the man was more polite to strangers. "Have a seat, and we'll let him know you are here." Boris sat down and ordered a drink. Yesterday Yankee had called and said they needed to talk. Boris didn't want Yankee coming to Brooklyn with all the unfinished trouble, so he said he would come to Washington Heights instead.

Yankee came out right away, and the two men hugged. "Come on back," he told Boris. All the men sitting at the last table agreed that Boris was an important person because Yankee only came out front to meet guests who were important. Less important guests were sent back to the office. Yankee's men noted this simple fact, making them more attentive to their duties.

Sitting down at a small conference table, Yankee poured Boris a drink. "Johnny is worried about you," Yankee said, not wasting any time. They were good friends, which meant they did not have to bullshit each other.

Boris laughed. "I know. Tell him not to worry; I am following his direction. I will kill that whole crew but not his precious Little Mike."

Yankee smiled back. "That is not fair, my friend, and you know it. Johnny could care less about this guy. I guess that Johnny would love to see Little Mike get whacked, but these are the rules he is bound to. It's the rules, not the person. You are much more important to us than a dozen little Mikes are."

Boris laughed again. "I know, I'm just busting balls. I am making things difficult for this Little Mike so he might reach out to Johnny again."

"Let him go where he needs to. Who cares?" The waiter came in with food, and the two friends spent the next hour joking, sharing news, gossip, and chances to make a score, and then finally eating. Boris particularly liked the rice and beans. He ate two plates of them and rubbed his belly. "I need a nap now."

"Johnny and I were just laughing at how old we are getting. Naps are good, aren't they, my friend."

"Oh yeah, as long as it ain't the death nap. I still got a lot of work to do."

***

Stephan got the call from Alex, the driver he had set free. The Russians wanted to meet but wanted it to be in a public setting.

"How many will be attending?" Stephan asked.

"There are only nine of us left. We all have men under us, but they will not be attending." They decided to meet on the pier at Coney Island. The meeting was set for two in the afternoon. Stephan showed up at two fifteen. He had been there since one but had been watching from a hidden location the whole time. When he felt there was no setup, he walked onto the pier.

"Gentlemen," he said with both hands in his pockets, "I am Stephan Elson. Who are you?"

Each man introduced himself, and Stephan shook each man's hand. "I am glad you called. There is no need for any more killing. After all, we are all brothers. Do you all agree that the Solnstevskaya Bratva here in New York is finished?" He waited for each man to confirm this. All but one did. Stephan looked at him. "And your name again, please?"

The man looked back at Stephan. "Michael."

"Michael, yes. And you do not concede defeat?" "I do not concede the Solnstevskaya Bratva is finished. We are here, and so it is not finished. We have all sworn an allegiance. How can we put that aside?"

Stephan liked that the man was speaking the truth from his heart. It would be a shame to kill him. He would try diplomacy first. "I agree with you, Michael, but the allegiance you speak of was for something no longer exists. Think of it as a merger rather than as a take-over. You nine men can't win if you continue to fight. And what are you giving up? Nothing! The twenty-five percent you were giving to the Italians will come to us instead." He looked at each of the men now as he spoke. "Each one of you men will be with me in my gang. You will keep whatever business you bring to the table and will have lots of opportunities to make more money with us. You all know who I am, yes?"

Everyone nodded their heads. "Good, then you know I would have no problem to kill any or all of you. But I wish not to. I'd rather you join me, and we do things together. Boris is our leader, and he is a good man. He did not start this war, as you well know. He only acted as anyone of you would have acted to fight to survive, win, last one more day, and keep his troops strong. I won't talk bad of the dead, but Boris is a much better leader than you had. He is a reasonable man, and he is willing to accept each of you into the Izmaylovskaya Gang as an equal. Michael, will you join us?" Michael looked at the others and then back to Stephan.

He nodded his head. "Yes. I will be glad to be with you on your team Stephan Elson." The two men hugged, and everyone clapped. "Come. Boris has a lunch set for us and will welcome you personally."

***

Another Tuesday meeting with the regime was finishing up. Johnny walked out of the social club in Harlem with Danny. "Where is Mario?" he asked.

Danny made a face. "He called me this morning and said he was sick and wouldn't be down. He's sending TD down with an envelope for the boss's legal defense."

"And?"

"And what?" Danny asked.

"Danny, we have known each other all of our lives. Don't play stupid with me now. There's more. I can read you like an open book. That's why you can't ever beat Nicky at cards! You wear your emotions on your sleeve, and you can't bluff worth a shit."

"I'm not getting good feelings from this fucking Mario. He told me he was seeing Joey Peanuts on Friday about some business they had, and he would give the envelope to him to pass on to the boss."

Johnny stopped walking. "He wanted to give the envelope to a different captain? Has he lost his fucking mind?"

"I know," Danny agreed. "I told him in no uncertain terms not to do that. That's when he said he would send TD down with it."

Johnny was concerned. That kind of move showed total disrespect for him as a skipper of the crew. What was Mario up to? He must be up to something. Otherwise, there was no way he would be so bold unless he wanted to send a very clear message. Even Danny sensed it. "Is TD coming down now?" Johnny asked as they began walking again.

"Yeah, he's supposed to. I guess so." Johnny nodded his head. "I wanna see him when he shows up. What else we got?"

"Everyone brought down an envelope. Looks like about forty G's. Nicky kind of pinpointed the spot Uncle Lenny called from. He said we can find it on a GPS."

"What does 'kind of' mean?" "It means he's pretty sure he has it figured out. I'm sending Gino, Charlie, and Joey to Little Rock with a GPS." "No, just send Gino for now. The three of them will stick out like sore thumbs out there. Have him fly into Memphis and drive down from there. Make sure he uses a fake I.D. with everything; tickets, rentals, whatever he does."

"What are you gonna do about Mario?" Danny asked as he smoothed his hair back.

"I don't know yet. I have to think about that."

***

They made love all afternoon on and off. Apollo didn't get dressed the entire day. As the sun was setting, he stretched and looked to his side. Micki was fast asleep. He watched her for a few minutes. She was beautiful, and their love-making was fantastic. He was really starting to fall for her. Apollo had never been married though he had three children. The thought of settling down with one woman had never appealed to him. Johnny would always say that 'guys like us, full-time gangsters, should never marry.' Apollo got out of bed and went to the shower. What the hell was the matter with him lying there thinking about marriage? He thought about Micki as he washed. She was beautiful, had a good sense of humor, and was classy and sexy all in one. He came out of the bathroom with the towel wrapped around him. Micki was sitting up in bed.

Looking down at her, he said, "Oh, you're up." Smiling, she replied, "In my sleep, I felt that you had gotten out of bed, and I woke up. The spiritual connection was broken. You should have awakened me. I would've taken a shower with you."

"I like solo showers."

"You might change your mind once we've taken one together," she said and winked at him.

"Where do you wanna go eat?" he asked. She looked at the bedside clock. "I don't have time. I have to go to work."

Apollo realized he didn't want to be without her tonight. "No, you just stay with me tonight. I'll call Donald and clear it for you."

"But I need the money, baby. The tips pay my bills." Apollo walked over to his pants that were thrown over a chair. Reaching inside the front pocket, he pulled out a wad of bills and ripped off two hundred dollar bills. "This should cover your tips for a Tuesday night." He reached out to give her the money.

"I can't take that from you, Apollo."

"Why not?" he asked, truly confused.

"Because it'll make me feel like I'm sleeping with you for money. It's just not right."

He sat on the bed next to her and smiled. "I want you with me. That's all it means. It's my way of having your company. I know you have to work for a living, but I want to be selfish and spend the night with you. So please take this and don't go to work tonight."

Micki smiled. She was really starting to dig this guy, and here she was setting him up to get busted. Oh

God, this was getting too much for her to handle. As much as she wanted to run, she wanted, even more, to stay in his arms. "Okay, since you put it like that, I have to go home first. I don't have any clothes to wear."

"Not a problem. Get dressed. We're going shopping." "What? Shopping?"

"Yeah, I want to treat you to a small shopping spree."

"Apollo, there's no such thing as a small shopping spree."

"Okay, then, a huge shopping spree." The joy and the guilt were too much for her. She sat there in bed, her head buried in her palms, and cried. She truly did not know what to do.

CHAPTER THIRTY-ONE

"So, how did it go yesterday? Did you follow Johnny?"

TD nodded his head. "Yeah, but nothing yet. After I dropped the money off to Danny, I went around the corner and met them," he said, pointing to the Conte brothers. "I figure if we follow him a few more times, we should have it down."

Mario was enjoying this. "You better do that without being spotted." The restaurant was full, and even though the four men sat near the back, they talked in low voices so as not to be overheard.

"We used two cars, switching back and forth, so we didn't stand out," Joe Conte said proudly. "And we stayed way back," chimed in his brother Guy.

"Good, very good. So have you thought this thing through?" Mario wanted to make sure this went down clean.

"You want us to snatch him, right?" TD asked.

"You'll have to because I don't want him gunned down in the street. That would leave too many questions that can't be answered. He needs to disappear. This can't come back on us."

TD waved his hand. "Don't sweat it. Everything will turn out as it should. It's under control."

"Don't get cocky on this one, Anthony. They don't call him 'Angel' for nothing. He's no fool, and he's a tough son-of-a-bitch. If you don't catch him just right, he'll put up a fight, so it has to be in a secluded place."

"You wanna come and say goodbye to him before we whack him, or should I just tell him this is from you?"

"What are ya planning on, having a conversation with him? Bake him a fucking cake? Listen, he's a made guy, a damn captain at that— just do him fast and as painless as possible. The least we can do is kill him with some respect."

TD laughed. "That's a good one. 'Kill him with some respect.'"

"Hey," Mario said and grabbed TD's arm. "Stop playing around. This is serious shit here— there's nothing funny about this. We're breaking all the rules here. If this doesn't go right, we're all dead." He shook his head like he was dealing with children not knowing when to stop playing.

TD put on a serious face. "Sorry, boss." He could see Mario was nervous. He was stepping way out of line and was feeling the pressure. TD could tell Mario was different and what he noticed for the first time was that difference—was fear. It was obvious that Mario was afraid. If he wanted to make a move like this, then go for it. But if he was afraid, then he should stand pat. Mario was not standing pat because he was hiding behind TD and the Conte brothers, hoping they would pull this off. TD realized all this and tried to make him feel better. "Don't worry, Mario; we got this under control. We won't let you down."

Mario shook his head. "I hope not," was all he said.

***

Little Mike had no idea who to contact. All of his Russians were dead. He knew there was still a crew of them, but he wasn't sure who they were or where they stayed at. He took Chilly and a couple of other guys to the club the Russians always hung out at, but no one there would tell him anything. "Who's in charge here?" Mike asked with an obviously bad attitude.

"I am in charge of the bar, sir," the bartender replied. "What is it you are looking for?"

"Who took over for Russian Paul?"

"I'm sorry, sir, but I do not know who Russian Paul is."

Mike wasn't buying any of that. "I suppose you don't know Georgie Z or Vip either?"

"Yes, Vip was my cousin. His wife owns this bar, and I help her run it, but I do not know what you are looking for?"

"Georgie took over for Vip. Russian Paul took over for Georgie. What I want to know is who took over for Russian Paul?" Mike asked as spittle came out of his mouth, and the veins in his neck bulged.

The man shook his head. "I do not know what you speak of taking over? We just have a bar here, nothing else." There were customers at most of the tables, and now they were all watching Little Mike with his loudmouth making a scene. Mike and Chilly were leaning against the bar, talking with the man behind the bar

"You see this man?" Mike asked, pointing to Chilly.

"Yes, of course." "He will be here on Friday to pick up my envelope. If no one meets him here with my envelope, then I will come back and take this bar apart—so maybe now you'll understand what I speak of."

"I am very sorry. I cannot help you, sir."

"Yeah, and Friday, if my money ain't here, I can't help you either." He nodded his head, and they walked out of the bar. When they got back in the car, Mike turned to Chilly. "If there's no money here Friday, smash the shit out of that place. Take me back to our joint. I'm disgusted." He slammed back in the seat and crossed his arms over his chest. Once Mike was back at his base of operations, he felt a little better. He couldn't help thinking that Johnny Angel was behind all this shit, and now he was reaping the benefits at Mike's expense. This was something he could not chew, let alone swallow. Mike was fed-up. He demanded his money. Moreover, he demanded respect—and if he didn't get the former, he'd take the latter.

***

He took the package from Donald and walked outside. He got in the back of the car that was waiting for him with two agents, and they drove off. "How did it go?" asked the agent in the passenger seat.

"Is my recorder not working?" Jerome had a fake cell phone that was a recording device.

"It is. I'm just making conversation."

"Oh shit, you had me worried for a minute. Yeah, everything is fine. I got a half a kilo."

The agent driving laughed. "We went from a quarter key to half a key in four days. These guys are easy." He laughed again as he drove off.

"He trusts me. He thinks I'm related to Apollo or something like that," Jerome said, full of himself.

"Speaking of Apollo, can we get him involved in these deals? Or do we need to flip Donald first and see where he takes us?" his supervisor asked.

Jerome thought about it for a moment. "I don't know; maybe I can thank Apollo for hooking me up with Donald. Do you think that would hold up in court?"

"No way," said the passenger. "You can't prove Apollo had any knowledge of what you and Donald are doing."

"He's the boss—he's got to know everything that happens here in Harlem."

The agent in the passenger seat was in charge of the case. "No, that won't cut it. We're going to have to go slow here, Jerome. This will take some time to get close to Apollo. It isn't going to happen in a week. So get back to work. Next week we'll buy a whole kilo."

"Okay. See you guys later." They pulled over at the next block so Jerome could get back to the club.

As Jerome was getting out of the car, the agent in charge said, "You're doing a great job, Jerome. Keep with it."

"Thanks." When he got back inside the club, Micki came up to him. "We have to talk," she said nervously. He looked around. "Let's go outside." He didn't want to risk anyone overhearing him. They both quickly headed back outside and

Micki started in right away. She leaned forward and said, "I can't do this."

Jerome made a face. "Are we going to have to go through this once a week? What part of this do you not understand?" he said in a harsh whisper, checking the surroundings to make sure no one was listening.

"I'm ready to go to jail. In fact, I'd rather go to jail than do this!" she responded in an almost desperate tone.

Jerome was slightly worried now because he saw the toll this was taking on her, but he had her back against the wall, and he wasn't going to let up. "And your grandma, is she ready to go to jail too?"

"I knew you were going to say that. To me, that makes you lower than any of these people you're trying to set up. No, my grandmother is not ready to go to jail, and I doubt if she would. She had nothing to do with any of my shit, and you know it." She crossed her arms over her chest and stamped her foot. She moved her hair out of her face and stared at Jerome.

"I don't know it, Micki, but I'm willing to take your word for it as long as you're helping us. I can see all this is getting to you. Maybe we need to get you away for a while."

"No, I want out of this whole deal. I can't do it."

Jerome got mad. "That's not going to happen, Micki." He stepped forward and put his finger in her face. "You are not walking away from this, and if you do, you and your grandma will be in a lot of trouble. Go home. I'll tell Donald you're not feeling well. Wait for me there, and we'll discuss this later." He hailed a taxi. Micki, obviously mad as hell, got in the taxi and told the driver the address. When the taxi pulled away, he pulled out his phone and called his agent in charge. When the agent answered on the first ring, he said, "We've got a problem."

***

The drive from Memphis to Little Rock took about two hours. It took Gino another hour to figure out the GPS and find the predetermined spot that Lenny had called from. It was a mall, and just like any mall in the United States, it was big and crowded. To Gino, they all looked the same. What the hell was Lenny doing here? Gino parked the car in the huge parking lot and got out. He stood and looked at the mall. If you have seen one, you have seen them all. He turned his back to the mall and looked at the surrounding area.

Across the street from the mall, was a smaller strip mall with about eight stores. On one side, there was a Thai food place, and on the other end, in the corner spot, was an Italian restaurant. Gino smiled. That was where

Lenny called from, no doubt about it. He got back in the car and drove across the street. He looked at all the stores. There was a Sprint phone store, a unisex salon, a tailor, a shoe store, a Starbucks, a bridal shop, and the two restaurants. The sign for the Italian place read "Pizza & Pasta."

He parked at the far end and walked back to the Italian place. The first thing Gino noticed when he walked in was rap music coming from speakers in the ceiling. There was a young black kid behind the counter and a Mexican-looking guy making pizza. Gino walked up to the counter and asked for a slice of pizza.

"We don't have pizza slices," the young black kid said.

"What do you mean you don't have pizza slices? You got pizza?"

"Yes," the kid answered.

"So cut me a slice."

"You have to buy the whole pizza," the kid retorted.

"Okay, what kind of pie do you have?"

The kid looked confused. "I'm sorry, but we don't have pie, only pizza, pasta, and sandwiches."

For a minute, Gino thought the kid was messing with him, but he realized the kid was totally clueless.

"What do you call a whole pizza?"

The kid had a blank look on his face. "A pizza?" he replied, really not sure that was the right answer.

"Just forget it," Gino said, amazed that this could really happen, and walked out. When Gino got back in his car, he started laughing. If this was where Lenny was exiled, he must be dying a slow, painful death already. He really didn't need their help. Let the old man rot.

CHAPTER THIRTY-TWO

Just north of Hong Kong on mainland China is the city of Shenzhen. The booming metropolis of four million people is a hotbed of Triad activity. Prostitution, gambling, smuggling, and drugs are plentiful. The Triad operates with permission from corrupt Communist officials. Cheng led JB down a narrow backstreet to a basement apartment. Inside, a bank of computer screens and huge hard drives that were set up as a commercial enterprise resided. It looked like nothing that might be seen in someone's apartment. The room was high-tech heaven, with the air conditioning whirring away to keep the temperature cool for all the latest technology and three computer geeks working at their stations.

JB smiled as he realized these Chinese computer geeks were just like American or Italian computer geeks. They all had that same despairing demeanor and cheap, wrinkled clothing. A well-dressed man, looking stylishly like a gangster, greeted them. The man had a small frame and beady eyes. He reminded JB of the old American actor Peter Lorre. Beady Eyes and Cheng hugged. Cheng turned to JB and said, "This is my cousin Dui. You can call him Joe." JB and Joe shook hands.

"We are all set up for you," Joe said in bad, broken English. Cheng said something to Joe and then turned to JB.

"I will translate so we do not have any miscommunications."

JB took out some papers that were folded up in his pocket. "These are the addresses we need to hack into. Once we get in, I will show you where to go to find what we need. Then I will show you how to transfer it out."

Cheng spoke for a few minutes to the geeks. Turning back to JB, he said, "We will sit and have some tea. They will break the codes quickly, so we will wait." They went into the kitchen area. The room smelled wonderful. Something sweet was baking, and there was a mint aroma in the air. A beautiful young woman appeared from a room beside the kitchen and served them hot tea and biscuits. Cheng smiled as he watched JB eyeing the young lady.

"Tonight, I will take you to one of our places where there are many women even more beautiful than this little flower."

JB smiled back. "That sounds like a great plan." Forty minutes later, the geeks announced they had successfully hacked into the Chase Bank hard drive. JB was excited as he and Cheng quickly made their way to the computer room and stared at the computer screen. It was the inner workings of the hard drive, so it didn't seem like anything special. JB told Cheng where they needed to go in the banking system computers, and Cheng directed the geeks. Ten minutes later, they found it. One-sixteenth of a penny, one-quarter of a penny, there were literally thousands if not millions of these leftover, unaccounted fractions in the system.

The geeks quickly started scooping them up and directing them to a special bank account. From there, they would be transferred again and again until they reached the private Cayman Island numbered accounts.

The fractions started adding up to quarters, half dollars, and then dollars. The dollars added up to hundreds, then thousands, and two hours later, they had transferred over four hundred thousand dollars, and they hadn't even dented the mountain of fractioned cents. JB had them switch to a second bank account, and the transfers started again.

He was amazed at the technology that was available today. They were seven thousand miles away, safe and protected in an anonymous building somewhere in a big city in China—practically invisible. Yet somewhere in a secure underground basement room in New York City, there were banks of computers, each the size of two huge refrigerators stacked in rows a city block long. They accessed these hard drives and just stole millions of dollars. That amazed him.

Six hours into the transfers, JB said, "That's enough." They had removed just over eight million dollars. "Is there a reason why we are stopping?" Cheng asked. JB smiled. "How much you wanna make in one day?"

"There seems to be plenty left," Cheng answered, not understanding why they wouldn't take it all.

"Yes. Hopefully, they won't notice for a good long while. If we wipe it out, they may get wise too soon. Tomorrow we need to hit the Bank of America, and then this place needs to be shut down for good. All this equipment must be destroyed. We will replace it in another location, so these gentlemen are not out of business."

Cheng realized the Italian was right. He bowed. "As you wish," was all he said.

JB smiled and patted Cheng on the back. "We just stole eight million dollars while sitting here sipping tea. Is that not enough for you?"

***

New Rochelle is a city located in Westchester County, slightly north of New York City, bordering the Bronx. It is the safest city of its size in New York and the fifth safest of its size in the entire United States. The population of seventy-three thousand makes it a comfortable, small-sized city. One of the seventy-three thousand people who lived there was a Yankee with his family. His million-dollar home was where his wife and children lived. Not many of Yankee's business associates even knew this house existed, let alone had seen it. Most people thought Yankee lived in Washington Heights, in his old neighborhood.

On this Sunday afternoon, a small gathering of friends and family was enjoying a barbeque on this beautiful summer day. Johnny was the last to arrive with Theresa and Angel. As soon as Angel said hello to everyone, she quickly stripped down to her bathing suit and jumped into the huge in-ground pool. There were about twenty kids in the pool. This was the first time since Johnny got home that all five of the men and their families were together. Boris was there with his wife, two sons, and daughter. Lee brought his wife, son, and daughter. Apollo was there with his girlfriend Micki and his daughter. And, of course, Yankee's wife and five children were there as well. The kids were all around the same age and had known each other all their lives. They all got along well and enjoyed playing together on these rare occasions.

All the children were sheltered from the life their fathers lived. None of them imagined they were anything but hard-working businessmen. The wives knew better but never dreamed of talking about it or even acknowledging it. Their place was to take care of the family, and they were happy to leave it at that. The five men sat together in their shorts and bathing suits outside the cabana house. Yankee had some family members there who occasionally came by and chatted. For the most part, the five men were undisturbed in their leisure. At some point during the day, each man would walk off with Johnny and report on what was happening. Since the biggest problems seemed to be with Boris, Johnny wanted to talk with him first.

As they walked off on a path that led to a slew of trees and a koi pond with a bridge going over it, Yankee said, "Oh, this is going to take some time. The crazy Russian is at it again!"

The others laughed. Boris filled Johnny in on everything that had happened. "Your Little Mike is steaming. He came to Vip's bar wanting to know who was in charge. When he did not get any answers, he said his man Chilly would be back on Friday, and he would take the bar apart if his envelope wasn't there for him. Chilly came back Friday, but we had too many guys there for him to act up. But I can assure you; he is pissed."

Johnny absorbed it all for a moment and then said, "Fuck him. Let him go see whoever he gotta see. There's not much he can do if he doesn't have a crew anymore. He's got no claim on nothing. Let's see what happens. Just be careful… Desperate men do desperate things." Johnny stopped to admire the Koi fish. "The good news is business is better than ever. We've got all the whore houses in Spain now, and the dope is almost non-existent unless it comes from us. Thanks to JB, we're the only ones with a steady supply. Of course, here in Brooklyn, we now have twenty-five percent of all of Vip's old crew and everything they do. That's the money Little Mike is looking for."

"Okay, sounds like you got things under control. Just don't let your guard down. Too many people have been hurt in a short period of time, and that can never be a good thing."

"I was just protecting myself, Johnny."

"Don't get defensive. I'm not saying you did anything wrong. I'm just saying a lot of people are worse off now—and that isn't good."

Boris nodded his head. "Yeah, you're right, but this couldn't be avoided."

"No problem. We'll deal with it." Johnny and Boris made their way back to the others.

"Can you still play, or are you grounded?" Apollo asked.

Everyone laughed, including Boris, who replied, "No, I can still play, but I just lost my allowance for a week."

That really had everyone cracking up. Johnny poured a large glass of iced tea and lit a cigarette. Yankee was smoking a huge Cuban cigar. "Okay, who's next?" Johnny asked.

Lee got up and said, "If you try taking my allowance, I will kick your ass. Don't fuck with Chinese Godfather." The men were laughing so hard that all the other guests were staring at them like they were crazy. Yankee was choking on his cigar. That was the funniest thing he heard all year.

Johnny just shook his head. Looking at the others, he said, "I've been dealing with this shit since we were kids. I should never have saved his life." Johnny and Lee walked off laughing. "Your JB is some piece of work. Did he tell you about the bank scam?"

"He just mentioned he was working on a good one with you," replied Johnny.

"Good one! That's being modest. Today, they took eight million from one bank. Tomorrow, I'm sure they will hit another bank for just as much."

"Wow!" Johnny said.

"That's not even the good part. The good part is the bank may never realize the pennies are missing!" Lee went on to explain the thing to Johnny.

"Wow. That's something. Damn sure is," Johnny said, shaking his head.

"That's what I call fucking ingenious, brilliant!" Lee said as they made their way to the Koi pond. Johnny shook his head again. "Who the hell ever figured that out?"

"Don't know," Lee replied. "But he's a damn genius."

They walked back over to the guys, and Apollo got up. "Why you gotta make the black guy last?"

Johnny laughed. "Too late; you're already last."

"What about Yankee?" he said, pointing to him.

"He ain't black like you, Apollo. He's brown. Anyway, I already spoke with Yankee. Sorry man, it's the back of the bus again for your black ass. So, this must be serious if you brought her here," Johnny said as they walked off from the group.

"I'm digging her. She's special."

"Wow! I never thought I'd hear you say that. Where'd you meet her?"

"She was working at the club."

"Have you checked her out?" "Damn, I knew you were gonna say that. What's there to check out?"

"Well, you wouldn't know the answer to that until you do it. I'm just saying, pal, if you think she's someone you're gonna have around, you need to know everything there is about her."

Apollo stopped walking and looked off to where Micki sat with the other ladies. He thought about Johnny's question… He was right. Johnny was always right. "You're right, man. I'll look into it." Apollo looked over to all the ladies and saw Micki fitting right in with them. She was looking their way, so he waved.

Micki waved back. She was thinking about the meeting that she had with Jerome's supervisor. After she left the club the other night, Jerome had called his supervisor, and he came over to the apartment. He was really pouring on the charm but was firm about her part in this thing. She knew her back was against the wall, so she conceded—at least for the time being. After the supervisor left, Micki made her mind up. She was going to tell Apollo everything, and she hoped he'd understand. She was having real feelings for him. At this point, she could no more betray him than she could betray her grandmother. Micki thought she had this figured out.

If Apollo was willing to play along like he didn't know anything, then she could beat her case, and Apollo would not jeopardize himself in any way. The whole sting operation would go nowhere, and they could not blame her. It seemed like a great plan. All she had to do was convince Apollo. She believed he was feeling her the same way she was digging him. She hoped that was the truth because she needed to get the courage to tell him, and that had to be done sooner rather than later.

She watched as Apollo talked silently to Johnny Angel. He was the focus of the F.B.I.'s whole case. They told her that Johnny Angel was the most dangerous of today's Mafia guys. Of course, she didn't know him, but the little time she spent in his company made him seem like such a nice guy. All the things they said about Apollo were hard to believe too. He was always a gentleman, and everyone seemed to really like him. It was a waste of time trying to convince herself that they were good, honest men. The only thing that mattered was they were good to her. If she knew how many men were dead on account of those five guys, she would have never believed it. This was, she thought, definitely an example of ignorance being bliss if ever there was one.

CHAPTER THIRTY-THREE

At six o'clock on Monday morning, the F.B.I. raided Sully's house. Instead of busting the door in, they just rang the bell. No one anticipated any resistance. Sully answered the door in his boxer shorts. "Armando Gullianni?" asked the lead agent.

"He's not here," Sully answered.

"Very funny, Sully," said the agent in charge. "You're under arrest. Please put your hands behind your back."

"You gonna arrest me in my underwear?" Sully asked astonishingly.

"Ah shit, take him upstairs and watch him while he changes."

"What did you expect at six o'clock in the fucking morning...me wearing a tuxedo?"

"Be nice, and don't press your luck," the agent replied. This was not the first time he had arrested Sully, but this time, hopefully, it would stick. "Don't you want to know what you're being arrested for?"

"Does it matter?" Sully asked. "What do I give a shit? Whatever you say, my reply is I didn't do it."

"You should give a shit because you'll be behind bars," said one of the newer guys on the squad. The old lead agent just shook his head. He knew the young agent was no match for an oldtimer like Sully. Sully looked the young man up and down.

"Yeah, and by tonight I'll be free—but you'll still be an ugly bastard."

"Get him dressed!" barked the old lead agent. The two other agents marched Sully up the steps to get his clothes on.

***

Sully's lawyer came to the social club in Harlem to see Johnny at one o'clock the same day. There were six guys at a round table playing continental—but Johnny was having coffee sitting on a couch. He looked at the lawyer and asked, "So what are they charging him with?"

"Right now, a few bullshit trumped-up charges, but basically, it's a fraud case."

Johnny laughed. "No shit! Sully and fraud! Sully and fraud go together like M & M's. What fraud?"

"That's the interesting part. They're saying Sully fixed last year's forty-two-million-dollar lotto that his nephew won. Apparently, they've been suspicious from the beginning."

"What do they got?" "They finally flipped the maintenance kid. He's saying Sully made him tamper with the ping pong balls."

"What?" Johnny was confused. "What the hell are you talking about?"

"The kid that does maintenance at the building where they draw the lotto. He said Sully taught him how to pick the lock where the balls were stored. Once he got in, he took thirty-three balls and, with a hypodermic needle, shot one cc of water in each ball, so when they did the drawing that night, the lighter balls floated up the tube before the ones weighed down with the water. The day after the drawing, the balls were stolen."

Johnny was still laughing. "That fucking Sully is a piece of work. You gotta love him."

"Yeah, he's a piece of work all right—and they're basing their case on just how much a piece of work he is. The fact that he's on the blacklist for all Las Vegas and Atlantic City casinos, not to mention the Yonkers Racetrack. They said he fixed every race there one night. That's impossible, isn't it?"

Johnny smiled. "Not for Sully. So what does it look like?"

"That's the interesting thing. They—"

Johnny held his hand up to stop the lawyer. "You already said that. How many interesting things are there?"

The lawyer raised his shoulders and said, "We're talking about Sully. There are many interesting things."

"Go ahead," Johnny said, conceding.

"I'm not sure they really want this to get out. The lotto brings in huge amounts of money. It wouldn't look good if the public knew it could be manipulated so easily. People might even bring suits to get their money back. This could be a giant mess. I think they'd like Sully to plead out. Of course, no one has said so yet, but that's my gut feeling."

"Well, then you need to play that card." Johnny was excited; he loved a challenge. "When you meet with the DA, let him know that this is bullshit and that you're gonna go to press because the system is broken, and they just want someone to blame it on blah blah blah. You get my drift?"

"Gotcha," replied the lawyer.

Johnny took a sip of coffee he had on the table before him. "Is he making bail?"

"I go to court at three. I'm going to argue that this is a nonviolent charge, and my client has health issues and all the toppings. I should have him out tonight. And

Johnny, would you tell Sully to stop having a pissing contest with the agents. Apparently, some rookie and Sully had it out. Sully called him an ugly bastard, and that just incites these kids."

"I'll tell him what you said, counselor. Thanks. Let me know if he needs anything."

***

By the third day, Gino was ready to pull his hair out. He wanted to call Danny and tell him he was coming home, but he had strict orders not to call anyone from Little Rock. Johnny himself had met with him and said no matter what, you do not call anyone in New York while you are there. They even took his cell phone from him before he left. Danny would go to a payphone and call Gino twice a day. Danny had already called this morning, so he wouldn't be calling again until tonight.

Gino wanted to go home. He had spent three days hanging around the mall and watching that damn so-called Italian restaurant. By four o'clock, he was hungry and was about to call it a day when Lenny showed up. Gino had been sitting in his car behind the wheel. He was thinking about his choices to eat. The last few days, he had been living on Wendy's and K.F.C. He was barely paying attention when a small Chevy pulled in front of the Italian restaurant. He watched as the driver, a man in his late thirties, got out, and then the passenger got out. Gino immediately recognized Lenny. He hadn't changed at all in the almost three years he'd been gone. He had the gait of an old gangster, one that was unique to "Uncle Lenny."

He always liked the old guy and was shocked when he heard Lenny had flipped. Too bad he had to kill him. Oh well, the old man asked for it. Gino was so excited. It was hard to stay put behind the wheel, but he would wait and follow him home. That was his mission, and he would see it through. What he really wanted to do was go into the lousy little phony Italian restaurant, out here in the middle of Elvis country, and blast both of them. His thoughts about killing Lenny would have to wait for the order. Gino was playing it smart and safe because Lenny was Johnny's uncle. He needed to make damn sure Johnny wanted his uncle dead and disappeared.

Just over an hour later, they came out and got in the car. There wasn't a lot of traffic like in New York, so it was more difficult to follow someone here. Gino stayed back far enough to not be seen but close enough not to lose them. After a few minutes, the car pulled into a driveway of a beat-up old house. Lenny got out and went inside. The driver backed out of the driveway and drove two houses away, where he parked and got out too. "Oh, having lunch with your neighbor, how nice," Gino said out loud to himself. He went back to his hotel and waited for New York to call with further orders.

***

The Raceway Diner was on Yonkers Avenue, right across the street from Yonkers raceway, where the trotters ran. Little Mike was at the track, so Chilly waited in his car till his boss came. Chilly was still whirling from the reaming he got on Saturday. When he came back and told Little Mike what happened Friday night at Vip's bar, Mike went off on him. If Mike weren't a made guy, he would have knocked the shit out of him. Mike called him a little bitch and a hundred other things. Chilly tried to explain that twenty armed Russians were waiting for him. He thought it was stupid of Mike to tell them when they'd be back. So he took the brunt of Mike's fury. Eating humble pie was not on his menu, so it didn't feel good at all. Now, as he waited for Mike to show up, he talked himself into having to take Mike's shit without hitting him. Chilly thought that if Mike touched him, then all bets were off. He'd lay him out and deal with the consequences later.

Consequences my ass; he knew that hitting a made guy was a death sentence. He watched as Mike pulled up and got out of his car. As he was walking toward him, as Chilly got out of his car, he thought, If you lay your hands on me, I'll kill you…but Mike was not in a crazy mood anymore. He must have won at the track.

"Okay," he said in a normal voice. "What are we going to do with these fucking Russians?"

"I don't know, but I don't wanna tell them when I'm coming back again."

The sarcastic remark was not lost on Mike, and he smiled. "I deserved that. Sorry I went off on you the other day. I shouldn't have sent you when they knew you were coming. Let's move on. We need to take the offensive."

"What do you have in mind?"

"I can't believe that Boris wiped all Vip's crew out. I don't believe that for a second. So the question is...where are the rest of the crew?"

"I think," Chilly said, "there ain't enough of them to fight Boris, so they're laying low."

"No," Mike shook his head. "What are they going to do, lay low forever? You know the old saying, Chilly: 'If you can't beat 'em, join ' em.'"

Chilly thought about that for a minute. It made sense. "Yeah, could be. So now what?" "So now that fucking Johnny Angel is going to have to kick something this way. The problem is he's a damn skipper now, so I'll have to bring my skipper to sit down with him." "So then you and Johnny won't have any beef between yous. That's good." They walked into the diner and sat at a table in the back. There were only a few tables occupied, but they would fill up after the last race. They ordered two coffees and looked at the menu.

Mike smiled. "Yeah, that's really good. I'm glad you thought that. It's exactly what I want everyone to think. If everyone thinks we buried the hatchet, then they won't look at me when his ass turns up dead. It'll be on record that we came to an understanding and that we have no beef."

"It's a good plan," Chilly said.

"No, it's a great plan," he replied, all smiles now. Soon he would have the pleasure of taking Johnny Angel out once and for all. He leaned in close to Chilly and said, "This is how we're going to handle it..."

CHAPTER THIRTY-FOUR

Max Hendrix was just an ordinary guy. There was nothing special about him. He'd never been in war, in jail, or had anything really exciting happen to him. He had lived a very dull, humdrum life. He didn't complain. That was just where he was coming from. Fact is, he did not even consider his life uneventful. He just thought this is as good as it gets, the wife and kids.

Max lived vicariously through others, mostly in movies or books. He was average in looks, height, and weight. He was the type of guy that you would not notice. Nothing about him stood out; he was almost invisible, which is why Lenny chose him. Lenny, going under his new name Mr. Rogers, lived two houses down from Max. Of course, Max didn't know Mr. Rogers wasn't his name; at least not until it was too late. Max Hendrix was thirty-three years old. He had a wife named Josie. They had two kids; Mathew was nine, and Susie was seven. He taught math at Little Rock Central High School.

In the summers, the family would pile into the old Winnebago, explore the backwoods, and look for places to camp and fish. Nothing exciting had ever happened to him until now. His life would be forever changed as a result of his friendship with his new neighbor, Mr. Rogers. Mr. Rogers lived alone in a small, old house. He moved to Little Rock a few years ago, and the Hendrix family—being good neighbors—reached out to the lonely old man to no avail. The house he bought needed a lot of upkeep and repairs. The yard was always filled with dead, dry leaves in the fall; the lawn always needed cutting in the summer; the driveway would fill with occasional snow that never got cleared until the warm weather came.

Most of the kids in the neighborhood were afraid of Mr. Rogers. They were even afraid of the house itself, thinking it was haunted. Crazy rumors would go around that Mr. Rogers was some kind of monster. In a neighborhood like this, when one of the neighbors has a pitch-black house on Halloween when all the kids would be out trick or treating, it sent a clear message to everyone: Stay away. He was reclusive and antisocial too.

In over three years, he had never talked with anyone on the block. About a month ago, the mailman accidentally left a letter at Max's house that belonged to Mr. Rogers. His address was Two Twelve Spring Street, and Max's was Two Sixteen. Max asked his son Matty to run the letter over there, but the child was paralyzed with fear. Just the thought of stepping on the monster's property was enough to terrify the young boy. It was kind of funny to watch the kid deal with his Boogey Man, so Max let him off the hook and took the letter there himself.

He intended to leave it in the mailbox, but something compelled him to ring the bell and give it to him personally. With his curiosity getting the best of him, Max rang the old man's doorbell. After a minute or two, when Max turned to leave, there came a graveled but strong voice from beyond the door.

"What do you want?"

Max explained who he was and why he was there. He was in a state of great anticipation. His adrenaline was pumping as he fell into the illusion of the neighborhood kids. He heard the locks turn and the doorknob being twisted. He was seized by the most insane urge to run. The door opened, and Max was face-to-face with the monster of Spring Street. They stood looking at each other for a moment.

With a shaky outstretched hand, Max said, "Hi, I'm your neighbor, Max Hendrix."

The old man looked at Max's hand and then back up to his eyes. Finally, the old man said, "Why are you shaking? Are you cold—or scared?" Max finally looked him in the eyes and caught the slightest hint of a smile there. He let out a nervous laugh and said, "I have no idea. I'm not cold, I'm not scared." Lenny extended his old, wrinkled hand and shook Max's hand. His grip was firm and strong, quite a paradox to how the old man looked. Feeling normal again, Max said, "I live two houses up."

"I know," Lenny said. "You have a nice family; you should be proud."

"Thank you, that's nice of you to say. I don't mean to be nosey, but I know you live alone here. Do you need anything?" Max was trying to be neighborly and trying to make amends for his earlier fears which, for some reason, had him feeling guilty. He seemed to consider Max's question for a moment, and Max saw his eyes go blank.

It was just a fraction of a second, but he saw the deep contemplation and then 'Mr. Rogers' came back, smiled, and said, "No thanks. But I do appreciate your asking." And then, out of nowhere, Max found himself asking, "I'm about to have a small barbeque. Would you like to join us?"

The old man smiled, and all the lines on his face merged. He reminded Max of the Chinese dog with a face full of wrinkles. Max was also mesmerized by the brilliance of his eyes. They were so alive; they seemed to belong to a younger man's face. "I haven't had a barbeque in so long," he replied. "It's a fantastic idea, but I don't want to impose... Maybe some other time." Max tried to assure him that it was fine and that his family would love to have him, but the old man would not come. Max said goodbye and went back home. Later that afternoon, after the barbeque, he thought he might drop off a plate to Mr. Rogers. The sun was setting, and it cast its shadow on the old worn house.

Max found himself once again ringing the old man's bell. This time, the door opened much quicker than before. "I brought you a plate," Max stated, holding it up as proof.

"You gonna stay out there with it or what?" Lenny asked, not so much sarcastically but more in jest. Max slowly entered the lair like he was on a hunting expedition. The front door gave way to the living room, which was dark, validating the spooky image the old man and his decrepit timeworn house had in the closely-knit community. He led Max to the clean, outdated kitchen, but void of any warmth or personal touch. The smell of coffee scented the air. "Have a seat," the old man said.

Max sat down at the kitchen table and placed the plate down in the center. As Lenny sat across from Max, he pulled the dish toward himself and pleasantly nodded his head. "You want a cup of coffee?" he asked. It sounded like a plea in his voice—like he welcomed the company.

"Sure, why not," Max replied. "I've got a little time."

"That's all we have, son," he said. The confused look on Max's face was obvious. The old man explained. "A little time, that's all any of us have is a little time."

"Oh, I get it. Well, it looks like you've had a little more time than a lot of others get."

"Eighty-five," he replied. "Two weeks ago."
"Well, happy birthday, Mr. Rogers." Once again, his eyes mesmerized Max with their brilliance. They seemed so alive—almost too alive for a little old man like his neighbor, Mr. Rogers. Max wasn't quite sure if that made any sense, but that's how it seemed to him. He also recognized the old man's eagerness for the company though he lived like a recluse.

"Do you have any family here?" Max asked. His facial expression changed just a little, almost unnoticeable, but Max was looking right at him when he asked and was able to distinguish the tension that crept into Lenny's face.

The old man shook his head slowly and said, "No."

"Where's your family?" Max asked, immediately regretting his intrusion into the old man's privacy which he obviously cherished.

The old man took a cigarette from the kitchen table, lit it, and inhaled deeply. "I spent my entire life, all these years, for what? I have nothing to show for it, no one to connect me to my past. Seems like such a waste. When I die, who will know? Who's going to be there to say 'I'll miss old Lenny'? It just seems like a terrible waste." The old man put his head in his hands and fought the emotions.

"Who am I, Max? What have I contributed to life? It seems to me that eighty-five years on this planet should have some connection to it—but I have none. No one even knows I exist…" Lenny looked away, tears filling his eyes. He took a deep breath, looked at his guest, and continued. "…but I used to. I once lived high on the hog and had a wonderful life."

And so began the friendship between Lenny and Max. Once a week, they would go out to eat for the past six months. Tonight, driving back from the restaurant, Lenny said, "Come over Sunday morning. I'll make breakfast. I got something for you."

"Breakfast?" Max said. "Do you know how to cook?"

"I'm Italian," the old man said jokingly. "All Italians know how to cook." "Yeah,"

Max conceded. "All Italians can cook and are in the Mafia, right?" Lenny laughed good and hard. It was the best laugh, maybe the only laugh he had in a long time. If Max only knew how close that statement hit home.

***

Johnny waited patiently all week to talk to Mario. Tuesday morning at the crew meeting, he had decided how he would handle the situation. He told Danny to bring Mario outside so they could talk. Johnny, Danny, and Mario walked up the block.

"So, Mario, what gives with that move with Peanuts?"

"What move, Johnny?"

"You wanted to give the envelope that I told you to bring to me to another captain?"

Mario was fuming inside that he had to answer to this fucking Johnny Angel. He had the audacity to question him like he was a child that did something wrong. It took all he had to keep his composure. "I didn't mean anything by that, Johnny. I was sick that week, so I couldn't make it here, but I knew I'd be seeing Peanuts on Friday, so I said I would pass the envelope off. That's all."

"Is there anything you're not happy with, Mario? Like maybe me being the skipper?" Johnny asked, staring at him as they walked.

"Listen, Johnny, do I think I would have been a better choice? Yeah, I do. But am I resentful over it? No. They chose you, and that's the way it is. Period. There's nothing else to discuss. No disrespect, but I've been around a lot longer than you. I should have got the nod, but what do I know?"

"All right, Mario, I just wanna make sure you're okay. If you ever need to talk with me, just let Danny know. I'll forget about the whole thing," Johnny said, being magnanimous with the insinuation that he could harm Mario if he chose to.

It took everything that Mario had in him not to explode. This kid was fucking with him, and Mario swore he would pay for it. To think he had ordered a painless death! He'd have to rethink that. Johnny deserved to suffer before he died.

Once they were back at the clubhouse, Johnny dismissed him. "Okay, Mario, thanks." He walked away. Mario did not bother to go back inside. He just turned and left. He knew T.D. and the Conte brothers were close by. They would be ready to strike any day now. He couldn't wait.

When Mario was gone, Danny said, "You know you provoked him talking to him like that."

"That's the idea, Danny Boy, that's the idea. Now, if there's nothing else, I have a sit-down with Sally and Little Mike."

"That's still going on with Boris?"

Johnny smiled. "Yeah, but now he's got to bring his skipper because he can't sit with me by himself. That's got to have him a little crazy. All right, I gotta run. See you later."

Johnny jumped in a cab and went down to Mulberry Street. They were meeting in a café owned by one of the made guys in the Lucchese Family. Johnny agreed to meet on their turf to give them a false sense of power. When he arrived at the café, both men were already waiting. They all shook hands, and Sally asked what he wanted to drink.

"An espresso, thanks." They made small talk for a few minutes. Sally and Johnny had not seen each other since before Johnny went away.

After an appropriate amount of catching up, Sally said, "It seems we got a problem with these fucking Russians."

"Exactly what problem are we talking about, Sally?" Johnny asked as he took a sip of his steaming-hot espresso, freshly made.

"Mike had a good crew there and was earning well with them. Now they all seem to be gone— except they ain't all gone. Your Russians took over, and now they have all Mike's old business. Did I leave anything out?" he asked Mike, who just shook his head.

Johnny opened his hands. "It's not that simple, Sally. What happened was your guys made a move to whack my guys. I'm sure they didn't run that by you, Mike, because I know you wouldn't okay that. But anyway, my guys turned the tables on them and came out on top. They made peace with your guys, and everything was fine. Then your guys broke the peace again and started another war. My guys got the upper hand again and wiped them out this time. If you have no crew left out there, Mike, it's not any of my doing." Johnny leaned back in his chair.

"Does it really matter who's doing it was?" Sally asked. "The bottom line is a friend of ours is out a lot of business that you now have." Sally let the sentence end, implying much more than he stated.

Johnny waited a few moments, then said, "I only get ten percent of their take, and that gets shared all the way up the line. If you want more money from my crew, I can't help you there."

"I was getting twenty-five percent," Mike said, a little agitated.

"I only get ten," Johnny said. He leaned forward with his arms on the table. "Again, Mike, if your crew is gone, how is that my problem?"

"Mike's crew is not gone, Johnny," Sally replied in a calm and pleasant voice. "They're just part of your crew now, and Mike's money is going in your pocket. We realize we're not going to make what we used to, but we still deserve a piece. After all, Johnny, it's not like we aren't friends." Sally was smiling because he knew he had Johnny cornered.

Johnny knew he couldn't refuse them. Now it was a matter of how much they would walk away with. He nodded his head. "Okay, let's start with the understanding that my family doesn't lessen its position because that I can't do. I'll speak to the Russians and try to get you five percent."

Little Mike did not wait for his captain to speak. "It's gotta be at least ten percent, Johnny."

"There's a handful of your guys left, Mike. I'll get you ten percent of what they earn but not ten percent of what the old crew used to earn. There's some business that used to belong to guys that are dead now. That business went to the victors. The guys who were left had a choice to either join my guys or fight it out. They joined, knowing they couldn't win anymore. They were allowed to keep whatever business they had. They have to kick twenty-five percent of that up to their new boss. I'll get you ten percent of that. Fair enough?"

Mike nodded and smiled. "I can live with that. These fucking Russians are crazy, ain't they? Thank you, my friend." Mike stood up and hugged Johnny. Sally got up from the table too.

"Thanks, my friend." They hugged and said their goodbyes. Johnny was glad he could make things okay. He had enough problems going on. It was nice to cap this one-off.

Little Mike was furious. He knew he played it off well where no one would suspect him if something happened to Johnny Angel. He'd get with Chilly later and work that out. Johnny Angel had no idea who he was messing with. Little Mike would show him.

CHAPTER THIRTY-FIVE

"Gin," Nicky said and laid his cards down. For what might have been the thousandth time in their long friendship, Danny threw the cards in the air.

"I can't believe how lucky you are. I just needed one card for gin!"

"You needed this four," Nicky said and turned over his discard.

"Son of a bitch! Sometimes I swear you're a fucking cheater."

"Yeah, whatever, just pay up." Nicky totaled the score. "You owe two hundred and thirty. Just give me two and buy lunch today."

"Fuck you. The way you eat, I'll just pay the thirty bucks." Danny went into his pocket and handed the bills to Nicky, who was grinning from ear to ear. Just then, Johnny walked into the social club.

"Let me guess. He's a lucky fucker, ain't he?"

Danny nodded his head. "You got that right. I just needed one card for gin. Do you believe that shit? And don't you know he was holding that card on me!"

"That lucky bastard," Johnny said, playing along with Danny. "Let's take a walk." Danny got up, and Johnny added, "You too, you lucky bastard."

The three men stepped outside the club so they could talk and get away from any listening devices the government may have there. "We got credit cards," Johnny told them, "but here's the thing; each card is a hundred bucks. There's no guarantee how much the card is good for. You might buy a card for a hundred and can't even use it for much, but you can always buy things for fifty or under, and the card should work. On the other hand, you might get a card with a five-thousand-dollar limit on it. No way to tell before we use them."

"What's the chance they have been reported already and come back stolen?"

"These are not stolen, Nick; they're counterfeit. Let's say the name on the card is John Doe. The real John Doe has his card in his pocket, so he has no reason to report the card lost or stolen. You got a few weeks to use the card cause once John Doe gets his bill, he'll see all these charges that ain't his, and that card will be dead. Let's put together a bunch of people we can trust and send them out shopping. We want to concentrate on gold and silver. Buy gold coins, one-ounce bars, and silver coins—things like that. Send them down to the diamond district on Forty-Seventh Street and then Canal Street too."

"What's their cut?" Danny asked. Johnny made a gesture with his hand. "Give them twenty percent of what they buy. If they buy fourteen hundred dollars' worth of stuff, they get two hundred and eighty bucks."

"Thanks," Danny said sarcastically. "I never would have been able to figure the math out on that one."

"I know, and you can never beat Nicky Black in a game of gin either." Johnny smiled and winked at him.

"Oh," Nicky said, "leave me out of this bullshit, please. When do we get the cards?"

"They'll be here tomorrow." Johnny went into his pocket and took out an envelope.

"You guys split this. There's a hundred large in there. JB made a nice score with Lee. I'm giving you a piece of my end."

Danny's face lit up, and Nicky was all smiles. The three men hugged. "You see Nicky? I told you it pays to know the boss."

***

Apollo, Ray, and Jessie James entered the club and went right to their table, waiting for them in the VIP section. The waitress came over to take their order. Apollo went into his pocket and pulled a fifty-dollar bill out. "This is for you, sweetheart. Go take care of the other tables and send Micki over here to take care of us."

She smiled. "Sure thing, Mr. Apollo. Thank you." She walked off, shaking her extra-fine butt hard to show them what they were missing. A couple of minutes later, Micki came over and kissed Apollo.

"Hello gentlemen, what can I get you?" Apollo smiled. "Now that's what I call service." They all ordered, and when Micki walked off, Donald came over. When he shook hands with Apollo, he said,

"Can we speak for a minute?"

"Sit down," Apollo said. "We can talk right here. Did you sweep the place today?" Donald nodded his head.

"Yeah—and we found a bug on your table." Apollo had Donald sweep for bugs every day; especially in the places where he would be. Since he always sat at the same special table, it was not hard to figure out.

Apollo looked at Ray and Jessie but spoke to Donald. "Did the cameras pick anything up?"

"No," he replied, shaking his head. "We had three different groups sitting here. I looked through the camera twice but didn't see anything."

"Do you know the groups that sat here?"

"The first was one of your guys. I think his name is Rick Butler. He sat here with his girlfriend for about an hour."

"Definitely wasn't Rick," Ray said. When Micki returned with the drinks, everyone stopped talking while she served them.

"Do you want something, Donald?" Apollo asked.

"No, I'm good, thanks." Apollo looked at her and smiled. "Check back soon."

She smiled and walked off. When she was gone, Donald continued. "Next group was some youngsters. They sat for a couple of hours. As soon as they left, two guys came that I had never seen before. They were friends of Jerome."

Apollo made a face. "Jerome? Micki's brother?"

"Yeah. He escorted them back here and sat them."

Apollo thought about that for a minute. Micki once told him that Jerome needed a job because all his friends were lazy, broke bums, and couldn't help him. Apollo thought it strange that a broke, jobless guy could have friends with money big enough to sit VIP. "Let's have a look at those tapes." They all rose from their table and walked through the nightclub toward the office in the back. They walked in, and immediately Donald sat down at the computer and started typing. A minute later, the screen showed the VIP section.

"Okay, here comes Rick and his girlfriend." They watched as the next group came and went.

"Those kids are from the neighborhood, aren't they?" Apollo asked.

"I know those kids," Jessie said. "They hang on 106th St. They're good kids." Jerome came next with two well-dressed guys. He led them to the table and called the waitress over. It all looked quite natural. The camera did not show the hands of the men at the table. The angle was off and the distance too far. Apollo did not like the looks of the two men. Something about them bothered him. Watching for a few minutes, he realized that their dress did not match their mannerisms. It's like they dressed for the part but couldn't play it off. It just seemed out of whack somehow.

"Can you zoom in?" he asked, leaning closer to the screen. "I can, but the picture gets distorted, and the angle ain't right either."

"Have a camera installed there that shows a close-up of anyone sitting at that table. Can you print that?"

"Yeah." "Good. Print me two copies of the one with Jerome in the picture. I got a couple of detectives that owe me one. Maybe they can help. I got a bad feeling about this."

***

Boris was not okay with the current situation. He didn't have to deal with Little Mike, but he did have to kick back to him through Johnny. As much as he loved and respected Johnny, he felt he owed Mike nothing. Maybe now he could get away with killing Mike and make it look like a dope deal gone bad. After all, everything was settled between them so the heat wouldn't fall on him. He'd put that on hold until the weekend was over. He had an important guest here, and he needed to concentrate.

Desmond was in from Tel Aviv, and Mikila was in from Berlin. Both men were his equal in their respective territory, but since they were here on his turf, they charged themselves to his care. He needed to act as the host and provide whatever they wished. He had Ivan and Maxim detailed to their security. Tonight, they would dine in midtown at the world-famous Russian Tea Room on 57th Street.

Johnny and JB would join them later for some drinks. On Monday, Boris and his two guests would fly down to Miami. Sol from Toronto would meet them there, and the Izmaylovskaya Gang would have their very first international meeting. At least Boris did not have to worry about security. That would be Avi's job since he was boss in Miami.

Mikila was the most powerful boss, having crews in Berlin, Paris, and Spain. One of the things they would discuss was the fact that Boris had taken over southern Spain and placed Ivan Borsky in charge there. Mikila felt like anything in Spain belonged to him. Boris felt confident that the others would support him with his request for southern Spain. Mikila and Boris had both served together in the former Soviet Special Forces, so they had a bond.

Johnny and JB came, and they all dined together. A meal at the Russian Tea Room was too good an opportunity to pass up. Neither Johnny Angel nor JB had any intention of passing up a meal at one of New York's most famous and finest restaurants. Mikila told stories of how Boris was selling Soviet machine guns to rebel forces, and when he was caught, he quickly convinced his captain to be a partner. They raised their glasses in salute to Boris, sharing a good laugh.

Johnny knew from past experience that it was hard to keep up with the Russians in the booze department. These men were hardened warriors from the streets of Moscow and the steppes of Mother Russia. They drank vodka like it was water. He warned JB, but he seemed to be holding his own.

At one point, Mikila said, "Boris, I want you to know that I will not oppose you on the southern Spain deal."

Boris nodded his head. "Thank you, my old friend."

Mikila wagged his finger back at Boris. "Just don't get any ideas about moving north." That brought another round of laughs. JB wasn't sure what he could do with

Desmond in Tel Aviv, but he was very anxious to meet with Mikila and break into the Berlin market. He wondered if he could tap into the German banking system with the same ease he had with the American banks.

After JB started talking, the Russians invited the two Italians to meet them in Florida. JB accepted right away. Johnny held his hands up.

"I've got too much going on here right now but thank you for asking." They talked and drank for another hour. When the meal was done, Johnny invited them to a private club. They exited the restaurant together and waited for their cars to pull up. None of them had the slightest idea that the F.B.I. was busy taking their photos in a grey, an anonymous van parked a safe distance away.

When Desmond entered the country, the F.B.I. was notified. They put a tail on him to keep tabs on where he went and what he did. The agent taking the pictures was an old-time agent with twenty years in the organized crime division. He knew everyone in the game, and when he saw this crowd, he whistled. From within the van, the agent said, "The Russian Mafia, the Naples Mafia, and the American Mafia are all having a fancy dinner at The Russian Tea Room, right here in the middle of Manhattan. Can't be a good thing."

The other agent was familiar with Johnny Angel. He said, "Yeah, and that's Johnny Angel. You can add the Chinese Mafia, the Black Mafia, and the Colombian cartel to that list."

"We need to report this right away."

CHAPTER THIRTY-SIX

Lee always believed that his destiny was to lead. As far as the street businesses were concerned, Lee had finally put a reliable crew in place, and for years now, he hadn't had much trouble. With the right people in place and the right police kept happy, his many activities ran like a well-oiled corporation. At least until the Yakuza came around, they were not living up to their end of the agreement.

They kept all the money from the games, and last night they threw out the Tong's representative in the Queen's gambling parlor. This was an affront, an unconscionable breach of etiquette.

Cheng, who never liked the deal Johnny made with the Yakuza, was the first to speak up. "We must wipe them out. No more turning the other cheek."

"Yes, Cheng. I am afraid you are right." Turning to Anguo, Lee added.

"Send thirty men over to Queens and thirty more to Brooklyn. Any Yakuza show up, they die. We will stay there in force until we have restored honor. These two-bit Japanese hoodlums will have to be taught a lesson."

Anguo hesitated. "If we shoot people there, the game will have to close."

Lee nodded his understanding. "If you can surprise them and take them hostage, you can eliminate them elsewhere. If not, so be it. After the heat dies down, we will move the game to a new location and start again. The gamblers will follow. The only important thing is to regain our honor."

"I always knew the Yakuza could not be trusted," Cai said. He spoke up for the first time. "We gave our word, and we kept our word. The dishonor lies with those that did not keep their word."

Lee looked around his opulent office. What a shame to be making millions but have to go to war over pennies. Sometimes that's just how it is— honor before money always. "So, we are all in agreement? We will war with the Yakuza?" Lee looked at Cheng, who nodded his head. Anguo agreed, and finally, Cai voted to war also. "It is settled then. The council has voted to war on the Yakuza. All the four hundred twenty-sixes and forty nines, along with our young Blue Lanterns, will fight. This will give us an opportunity to initiate some of the outstanding Blue Lanterns."

"I knew this day would come," Cheng said. "I had some of my people follow Johnny Chu."

"Who is this Johnny Chu?" asked Lee.

Cheng smiled. "He is their leader—and I know where he lives."

"You have always been wise beyond your years, Cheng. Take Mr. Johnny Chu out today. That will cause confusion amongst the rest of them."

Lee stood up, and the others followed suit. It was time to go to war.

***

Apollo went to his office and called detective Martin Jackie. "What can I do for you, Apollo?"

"I was hoping you'd wanna repay the debt. I need a favor."

"You mean half of the debt. We still haven't caught the other kid." "True that, but I believe that Mr. Larry Hamilton gave you a full confession. He knew that one option was to deal with us. He considered his options carefully and chose to deal with you rather than us. So not only did we give you the guy, but we also got you the confession."

"What do you need, Apollo?" Detective Jackie asked, silently conceding.

"Can we meet?"

"You wanna come to my office?"

Apollo laughed. "Yeah, that would look great, wouldn't it? I was hoping you could come to mine." Detective Jackie had nothing really important to get done, and his curiosity was getting the best of him.

He said, "I'll be there in the next half hour."

"Thanks." Apollo hung up and considered the situation. It sure seemed like Jerome's friends hid the bug, and that could only mean one thing. The question that puzzled him was, where did Micki fit in all this? Was Jerome really her brother? They had different last names, but that could be easily explained; same mom but different dads or vice versa. Apollo sat at his desk and leaned back in his chair, contemplating the whole situation. Something wasn't adding up. He was starting to really dig Micki. Hopefully, that will continue.

Twenty minutes later, Detective Jackie was sitting in his office. When he sat down, Apollo said, "Can I get you something to drink?"

"No, thanks. I'm good. Tell me what's up."

Apollo opened his desk drawer and pulled out the bugging device they found. "We found this on the table I usually sit at." He went back into the drawer and pulled out the picture printed from the computer, and slid it across his desk. "We believe these three men might have planted it. Do you know anything about this?"

Martin Jackie shook his head. "I'm with homicide. They don't share information openly with us." As an after-thought, he added, "In fact, they don't share shit with us." He picked up the bug and looked it over, and then looked at the picture. "I'd say you got the Feds on your ass from the look of things here."

"Anyway, to find out about this guy here?" he asked, tapping on Jerome's face in the photo.

"I can't interfere with a federal investigation, Apollo. In fact, why don't I just pretend that you did not ask me that question and I didn't hear it? That would be way over my head—not to mention against the law. We're even."

"So you're sure it's the Feds?"

"Not a hundred percent, but if I were a betting man, that's where my money would be. The department certainly doesn't condone your behavior, but we're not stupid. The situation here would be a lot messier if you weren't running things. You know the deal: 'Get along, go along.'"

"Thanks for your time. I appreciate it." Detective Jackie stood up and offered his hand. Apollo shook it.

"Be careful, Apollo. Even you aren't immune from the Feds." When Detective Jackie left, Apollo thought about his next move. He knew Lee had some connections in the force. He told Cecil and Ray to have the car downstairs in five minutes. They were going to Chinatown. Apollo called Lee while they were on the way downtown. Lee gave him the address to a new jewelry store he opened on Canal Street. When they pulled up, Apollo was impressed at all the gold sitting in the store window. If someone smashed the store's display window, they could easily grab hundreds of thousands in gold. Apollo laughed, realizing what everyone else in the neighborhood already knew. No one would ever smash that window because it was an instant death sentence, one that would surely be carried out in a gruesome, public fashion.

As soon as Apollo entered the store, Lee came out from a back room as if on cue. The two men hugged hello, and Lee said, "What can I help you with, my friend?" Over the years, Johnny Angel had treated each of the four leaders with respect and had always preached that they should all be looking out for each other. The five men became like family— although an odd one. More like separate fingers on a hand. Together, they formed a strong fist. Each had sent their troops out for the others on different occasions.

Apollo explained the problem. He handed Lee the bug and picture. "You got anyone that can help?"

"Yeah, I think so. You said this one is your girlfriend's brother?" Lee asked, pointing to Jerome.

"Yep."

"Leave it with me. I'll see what I can come up with. Have you told Johnny yet?"

"Not yet. I'd like to know some more before I go to him."

Lee laughed. "As much as we love him, sometimes it's like going to your parents after you screwed up."

Apollo smiled. "I couldn't have said it better, Lee."

CHAPTER THIRTY-SEVEN

The July sun hid behind black clouds as hail the size of ping pong balls crashed down from the summer sky. Johnny Chu did not heed these ominous warnings as he pulled out of his garage and down the driveway of his Queens home. Like his Yakuza brothers, he hid in plain sight amongst the many Japanese immigrants, newly arrived. He did not seek to stand out, only to blend in. His safety was in his invisibility. He turned right onto Queens Boulevard and pulled into the gas station to fill up his fairly new Lexus. He ran to the shelter of the gas station, trying not to be pelted by the painful hail. He held his suit jacket over his head.

When he came out again, he held a paper over his head to shield the hail. His head was reasonably dry, but the rest of him was soaked. He danced between the slimy puddles, all mixed with gasoline, oil, and rainwater that almost came up to his ankles. It was, he decided, impossible to stay dry in a deluge like this one. He was so intent on filling up the gas tank and the hail that he never noticed the two men walk up to him. Johnny Chu had no idea that there was a problem at the gambling parlor. His men were waiting for him at their hang-out. They were going to inform him that Coffe went off on the Tong operator, throwing him out of the gambling parlor.

No one anticipated that Lee would retaliate so quickly for this grievous insult to the Tong. As a result, Johnny Chu was not prepared for an attack. The two shooters got a few feet away and opened fire. A headshot dropped him, and a few insurance rounds finished off the already-finished leader of the Yakuza. His blood mixed with the rain, hail, and oil as Johnny Chu lay dead on the ground. The two shooters got away easily in the storm. They parked the stolen vehicle a few blocks away and melded into the urban bustle. Once they were clear, they called Cheng.

When Cheng hung up with the shooters, he made another call. He had a hit squad outside the hang-out of the Yakuza waiting for his instructions. It was a short call. The only thing Cheng said when the phone was answered was: "Go."

Coffe had just arrived at the corner where the Yakuza clubhouse was, close enough to see ten men rushing the place. A second later, there were repeated thudding noises coming from inside. Coffe knew the sound of silenced weapons. He turned and walked away. Inside, eight Yakuza were completely taken by surprise as the Tong assassin squad struck. None of them ever had a chance to arm themselves as they were mowed down. Thunder roared as the black sky shook the earth and screamed mercilessly. Bodies fell like the hail outside, the roar of the gunfire muted by the roar of the thunder in the summer squall.

Coffe made his way to the Queen's gambling parlor. There were Tongs everywhere. Before any of them knew who he was, he began to fire. He knew he could not win, but he had vowed to himself that he would take a few Tongs with him before he died. He was full of guilt over the loss of his dead brothers. He had a little too much to drink last night and just lost it. He figured today he would hear from the leader, but he never expected all these killings. He instantly shot two men and then a third. Then he felt a burning somewhere in his side. The pain was intense, but he was still standing. He dropped another Tong and then was hit three more times.

Coffe fell, still shooting wildly, dying, but not defeated. He tasted the blood seeping out of his mouth and closed his eyes. Now he could go, content that he had exacted some revenge. Three Blue Lanterns lay dead along with the troublemaking Yakuza. The storm let up some as sirens sounded in the near distance. It was a short-lived war.

***

The four men stood around in a small circle in front of Mario's car at the White Castle burger building. The storm had passed, and the sky was clear. The smell of wet grass and summer was in the air. Mario was anxious to hear what was going on. "Are you guys ready on this thing or what?"

TD lit a cigarette and took a deep drag. "Yeah, we're ready. On Tuesday's after he's done with you guys, he usually goes to his girlfriend's place in Spanish Harlem and doesn't come back out for a couple of hours. We think we can snatch him up, walking into his building. It's the kind of neighborhood where people mind their own business. It's a good spot."

"Okay, then what?" "Then we take him upstate and bury his ass— unless you wanna see him first."

Mario was agitated. "What the hell do I want to see him for? You think I want to gloat over this? You think I like whacking my captain without permission?"

"No problem, boss. When we're done, I'll come and see you. Where will you be?"

"I got to go see the Irish pricks on Broadway, so meet me at Van Cortlandt Park Bar at the end of the train stop. Anthony, I'm counting on you to make this right. Don't disappoint me."

"Do I ever?" TD replied with a smile.

Turning to the Conte brothers, Mario said, "Don't disrespect this guy. He needs to die, but he's a man of honor, so treat him that way. I don't want you to abuse him. Just shoot him in the fucking head and bury him. Quick and painless, you understand?"

Guy and Joe both nodded their understanding. "What if he puts up a fight?" Joe asked.

Mario rolled his eyes. "How can he put up a fight? You get the drop on him, tie his fucking hands behind his back, take him upstate, shoot him in the fucking head and bury his ass. Where does 'put up a fight' fit into this?"

"I'm just asking," Joe replied as he shrugged.

"Well, don't ask stupid questions like that. It's not an option that he has a chance to fight." Then, turning to TD, he added, "Make sure you're on top of this, Anthony."

"Got it, boss, don't worry about a thing." Mario shook his head and walked away. He got in his car and drove off without saying another word. His mind was already past the Johnny thing. He was thinking about being the next skipper.

***

"Ah, come in, Stephan, sit down. Do you want a drink?"

"No, sir, thank you."

"Stephan, are you earning enough money working for us? I want you to know how important you are to this Brotherhood." "I have nothing to complain about, sir."

Boris waved his hand at Stephan. "Stop with the sir, already. It's me, Boris. I have a delicate job for you. All of Vip's old crew is under you now, correct?"

"Yes, sir."

"Who is the one that was reluctant to join with us?"

"That would be Michael, sir."

"And what is your take on Michael? Is he truly with us or just playing along?"

Stephan did not need to contemplate this question at all. He replied instantly, "Michael is a man of his word, sir. If he did not truly want to join, he would have fought until death."

Boris shook his head. "That would have made him a foolish man. Is he that stupid?"

"No, sir."

"Then he would not choose to die. He would join us instead. Can you be certain of his loyalty?"

"Yes, sir. I believe he is one hundred percent."

"Good. I want him to betray us. Not really, of course. I want him to seek out Little Mike and act as if he's upset that I have taken over. The point is he needs to befriend the Italian, so he gains his confidence. The best way is to make Little Mike earn some money with him."

"What is his goal?"

Boris laughed. He looked over at Maxim and then back at Stephan. He held his hands out, palms upward. "To kill him, of course. What better goal could a man like me have?"

CHAPTER THIRTY-EIGHT

The lovemaking was fantastic. Her body was perfect, her skin as smooth as silk, soft as butter, sweet as honey. He lay back on the pillow, and Micki lay on his chest. "So, how's your brother doing at work?" he asked.

"I guess okay," she replied.

"You guys don't look alike. Do you have the same dad?"

"Different dads," she replied. Micki started to tense, which was not lost on Apollo. A lifetime in the streets, in the rackets, made Apollo a very astute observer of human frailties. He smelled them like a dog on the trail of a kill—sometimes from miles away. It was his secret weapon.

"But you guys grew up together?"

"Not really." She looked up at him. "Do we have to talk about Jerome?"

"Why, is there something wrong?" Apollo thought she answered "no" a little too quickly.

"I'm sorry. I'd like to spend my time with you chillin' and not talking about Jerome," she said as she put her head back on his chest.

"Well, to tell you the truth, I thought since he's my woman's brother, maybe I should give him some other things to do. You know, like a promotion—maybe a little bit more serious work. What do you think?" Apollo was casting bait on the water, fishing to see exactly how far Micki would vouch for him.

"Apollo, I sent Jerome to see you, but if he doesn't work out, that's on him. I would take it slow before you give him anything serious, but please don't tell him I said that." And as an after-thought, she added, "I just don't want to fight with him. You understand, right?" she said, looking up at him once more.

"Yeah, no problem. I was just trying to look out for you."

She smiled and said, "Well, let me see if I can look out for you," as she slid down the bed and took him in her mouth. They stayed in bed for another hour and then showered together. They composed themselves and then headed down the street to a little soul food restaurant. Micki was so full of guilt that she could hardly stand it. She knew he sensed something, but he wasn't pressing it.

"Apollo," she said, sick to her stomach with this problem. She was starting to sweat. She was getting dizzy. She was not cut out for this stupid undercover police-type shit. She knew she couldn't do it much longer. "I need to tell you something, and I'm sure you're

318

going to hate me—but I'm starting to fall in love with you."

He stopped eating and looked at her. He was having the same feelings, and he knew what she was about to tell him was not going to be good. "Is it about your brother Jerome?"

She nodded her head. "He's not my brother…" She hesitated and took a long inhale, followed by an even longer exhale. She centered her eyes back on him. "He's an F.B.I. agent."

That took Apollo by surprise. He had figured Jerome was an informant, not an agent. That made things a little more difficult.

"Go ahead. Explain this, please," he said as he clasped his fingers together and leaned on his knuckles against the table. And she told him the whole story. How they threatened to lock her grandmother up and how the whole thing was meant to get Johnny Angel. "I'm going to tell them to lock me up. I'm sorry I put you in trouble, but I know I can't go on with this anymore. I'd rather do my time than ruin everyone else's life. I hope you can forgive me. Maybe when I get out, I can see you."

She was in tears, and Apollo instinctively knew she was on his side one hundred percent. "Hold on a minute, would you? I don't see why you have to go to jail. You did your part. You got Jerome on the inside. We can just keep him there and make sure he doesn't come up with anything. Then, they have to honor their deal with you."

"He already has come up with something." She hesitated before adding, "He's been buying coke from Donald."

***

Over the years, Johnny had set up an emergency code for the men to use. It was a simple code that meant a secret meeting was needed right away. The caller would identify himself with a sports game. Lee was tennis, Boris was soccer, Yankee was—of course—baseball, Danny was football, Nick was hockey, and Apollo was basketball. The place was also coded. Brooklyn meant the Bronx, the Bronx meant Brooklyn, Queens was Manhattan, Manhattan was Queens, Staten Island was Yonkers, and Yonkers was Staten Island. The call always had to be from a payphone. The name the caller used was irrelevant. If at all possible, the caller would get a stranger to speak after he dialed the number.

Shortly afterward, Apollo dropped Micki off at work. He reassured her and told her to act normal, to make like everything was okay. He had asked this older woman from the electronics store to speak on the phone for him. He told her exactly what to say. He immediately took her to the corner pay phone and called Johnny.

"Hello," Johnny answered. The woman spoke slowly, not wanting to screw the message up. To do a simple favor like this for Apollo was a delight. After all, he did for the neighborhood. "Yes, hello, this is Ellen from the basketball team you said you would sponsor."

"Yes, Ellen, how are you?"

"Fine, thank you, sir. We are having a meeting about fundraising tomorrow morning at nine at Brooklyn High School. Can you make it?" Tomorrow morning at nine meant the meeting was for nine tonight.

Johnny looked at his watch. It was seven forty-five. "No, I'm sorry, I have appointments in the morning, but please count me in for a small donation. Say, two hundred dollars." Johnny's answer was also in code. He said "no" he can't make it, followed by he would make a donation—which meant "yes," he would be there.

"Oh, thank you so much, sir. Have a nice evening." "You too, Ellen. Goodnight."

Johnny hung up and wondered what kind of trouble Apollo was in. Oh well, he'd find out soon enough. He left the building and walked the few blocks to the social club. Nick was shuffling the cards as Johnny walked in. "What's the score?" Johnny asked. Nick looked down at the sheet. "Eighty-seven to twelve." "Hurry up and finish him off."

Danny turned around in his chair. "I can't hurry, Johnny. This is a game of skill."

Johnny laughed. "I wasn't talkin' to you, Danny." After three picks, Nick knocked and caught Danny with forty-five more points. Danny threw the cards in the air and got up. Johnny nodded to Nicky also.

All three men walked outside. "I got a distress call from Apollo. Need to meet him on Westchester and Morris Park Avenue in the Bronx. I need you guys to get up there right away. Bring a few guys with you. Stay back and keep an eye on everything. If I go like this…" Johnny put his hands behind his neck and stretched his head back. "you come to me. If I do this…" Johnny put his left hand on his right shoulder and swung his arm around in a circle, "then you stay back and follow Apollo. Got it?"

Danny and Nick nodded and immediately gathered up four guys quickly and headed up to the Bronx. By the time Johnny got there, the others were in place but not visible. A couple of minutes after nine, Apollo pulled up. He got out of the car and headed over to Johnny. The two men hugged hello. Apollo started to tell Johnny the whole story.

"I knew something was wrong. I went to see Lee after the detective I knew said he couldn't help."

"What did Lee say?"

"He hasn't gotten back to me yet."

"I think your plan with the girl will work—but you got a problem with Donald. You have to move quickly on that but be extra cautious. They might be watching him or even flipped him already. He has to disappear and never be found. Get one of your guys to use his identification and fly into Jamaica. Then he should fly to the Bahamas with his own I.D. and from there back home. If they try to track Donald, they'll trace him to Jamaica. They will think he took off."

Johnny put his left hand on his right shoulder and swung his arm around in a circle. "My damn shoulder is killing me. I think I slept wrong on it," he told Apollo.

Nick and Danny got the message. Nick would follow Apollo, and Danny would lag behind to see if anyone was following them. "I'm gonna go down and see Lee. Maybe he's got some info. You go hang out at the club. I'll come through there on my way back." Johnny said and placed his hand on Apollo's shoulder. "Don't worry, pal. We'll make this good."

"You're going to come to the club?" Apollo asked with incredulity.

"Yeah," Johnny smiled. "They want to make a case on me. Let them think they're getting somewhere." Two hours later, Johnny made his way to the club. There was a small line out front. Johnny bypassed the line and started for the front door. Jerome was on duty. He recognized Johnny right away but played like he had no idea who he was.

"I'm sorry, sir, but there's a line here. You'll have to get in line."

Johnny knew that was Jerome from the picture Lee showed him. He bit his tongue to keep from laughing in the agent's face. "I don't wait in lines, pal," he said. "Now, if you wanna keep your job, get your boss on that little secret service walkie-talkie thing in your ear."

"Who should I say is here?" Jerome asked.

"I don't care what you tell him, boy. But if you don't get out of my way, I promise you; you won't have a job in five minutes." Jerome thought for a moment. He didn't want to give them a reason to fire him, so he didn't want to press it too much.

"I don't work for you, sir. You can't fire me." Johnny walked around Jerome and inside the door. "Get out of my way, asshole."

Jerome ran in behind him. Johnny was waiting for Jerome to touch him so he could knock him out. He knew he wouldn't blow his cover over getting knocked out, and the fact that Jerome touched him first meant it couldn't be assault. Just as Johnny figured, Jerome ran up behind Johnny and grabbed his left arm. Johnny turned around and knocked him flat out with one shot to the side of the face.

The inside doorman saw the whole thing but couldn't act quickly enough. "Sorry, Mr. Angel, he's new."

Johnny had a big smile on his face. He looked at the bleeding, slightly conscious Jerome on the ground. "Yeah, well, then I won't step on his head." He stepped over the F.B.I. agent's prone body. He could hear the din of whispers from the dozens of people who witnessed what anyone would consider a very ballsy move made by this middle-aged white guy in the middle of Harlem. Johnny walked into the main area of the club. He quickly saw Apollo waiting for him at his V.I.P. table.

"What are you all smiles about? You look like you just smoked a joint," he asked Johnny.

"No," Johnny shook his head, "but I did smoke your F.B.I. agent." He told Apollo what had happened.

Apollo laughed. "You planned that whole thing, didn't you?"

"I played him like a cheap violin." Johnny's grin took over his entire face. Just then, Donald came to the V.I.P. table, bringing Jerome by his arm and pushing him forward.

Donald came right over to Johnny. "I'm so sorry, Johnny. He's new here. He didn't know who you were." Johnny thought he'd have a little more fun. He looked over at Jerome, who had a nice size knot under his left eye where Johnny had hit him.

"Come here, boy." Jerome came over. His eyes were blazing with anger. This son-of-a-bitch was calling him 'boy'! He couldn't wait to snap the cuffs on him. Johnny looked at him. He knew Jerome was pissed. "What do you got to say for yourself, boy?"

Jerome hesitated. "I'm sorry, sir. I didn't know who you were," he mumbled while averting his eyes, keeping his anger in check.

"You wrinkled my jacket, boy. You gonna pay for my jacket?" he asked, pointing at the wrinkled lapel.

"If I have to, sir," Jerome replied. He did not want to blow it and lose his job there.

"You got seven hundred bucks on you, boy?" Jerome swore if he called him a boy one more time, he was going to lose it.

"No, sir," was all he said.

"Maybe I'll let you shine my shoes. In the meantime, get the fuck away from me before I smack you again." Jerome turned and stomped off. Everyone was watching Johnny humiliate him. Jerome would count the minutes, waiting for the moment to come when he could get even with this arrogant gangster prick. When he walked off, Apollo laughed like crazy.

"Oh man, that was beautiful! So, what'd you find out?" "What you already know. The three of them are agents, and that's an F.B.I. bug for sure. That was all Lee was able to find out."

"That's plenty. Damn Johnny, I wish I recorded that; it was priceless. Like that stupid commercial. You are the best."

Johnny got serious. He leaned over and whispered, "Be careful with Donald. Make sure he's not wired before you whack him, and do it quickly. You have to make him disappear. No body, no murder. No murder, no crime." Apollo nodded. No need to reply.

CHAPTER THIRTY-NINE

"Tito, this fucking thing is not working!" Yankee yelled. Tito walked into the room they used to count money and shrugged his shoulders.

"What am I, the fucking Maytag repairman?"

"Puta," Yankee said. He was disgusted with the whole situation. "Come on, figure something out, would you? We got twenty boxes of fucking money! What are we gonna do, count it by hand? You are in charge of the money, right?"

"Yes, Yankee, I am in charge of the money— but I don't know how to fix a money-counting machine." "We have a multi-million-dollar business, and we only have one machine to count money? That doesn't make any fucking sense."

"We had that big machine the Feds took when they raided the house on Long Island last year, remember?"

"Where are George and Juan?"

"Downstairs. You want them?"

"Can they count money? Yes, Tito. I want them. We have to count this fucking money. I need to have it boxed up and ready to go." Tito took out his phone and called George. A few minutes later, George and Juan came into the apartment. Yankee looked at them. "Do either of you know how to fix this machine?" Both men said they did not. Yankee was fed up. "It will take us all night to count this money, so let's get busy."

"Hold on," George said. "I know what to do. I'll be right back." George left, and five minutes later, he walked in with two triple-beam scales. In the same building on a different floor, they had an apartment where they bagged up the dope. They had a dozen triple-beam scales there. He put them on the table and turned one on. It was the new digital model. "There, that will work!"

"What am I supposed to do with a fucking scale?" Yankee was losing his patience at this point.

"Weigh the money," George answered. "Each bill is one gram." He looked pleased with himself. Yankee relaxed a bit and smiled, immediately taking a handful of the twenties and slapping them down on the scale. It read seventy-two grams. He did the math in his head. "What's that, fourteen hundred and forty bucks? Okay, so five hundred twenties is ten thousand, right?"

The three men just agreed, not being completely sure. They had three big boxes filled with the twenties, five boxes filled with tens, eight boxes filled with fives, one box of each fifties and hundreds, and two boxes filled with ones. A few hours later, they were finished counting the money. It was just over five hundred thousand. "Okay, so now you know how to do it. I am going out to have some fun."

All three men complained. "I don't wanna hear it!" Yankee declared. "Find a damn counting machine before next week, or you'll have to do this shit all over again." With that said, he left.

***

It was a beautiful summer day. The daily hustle and bustle of the city were in full swing. Ray went to a payphone and called Donald. After five rings, Donald picked up. "Get in a cab. I'll call you and hang up after one ring. Then you have the cab pull over and get out."

"Okay," Donald said. He knew that was Ray. These guys were always so cautious; sometimes, it was annoying. He left his building and hailed a taxi. Ray followed the cab from a safe distance. After he was satisfied there was no tail on Donald, he rang his phone once and hung up. He watched as the cab pulled over and Donald got out. He pulled up right away, and Donald jumped in. Ray swung back into traffic.

"Hey, big Don, how you doing?" he asked him.

"You know me, Ray. I can't complain. What's up?"

"I have no idea. I don't ask questions some meeting about something,"

Donald said. "Well, his timing sucks. I was going to my little hot Latin mama's place for some afternoon delight."

"Give me the address. I'll drop you at the meeting and then go take care of that for you, keep everybody happy," Ray said jokingly.

Donald laughed. "She got a friend. When you pick me up on the way back, come in for a minute. You can meet her, and I'll tell her to hook you up."

Ray let go of the wheel for a moment and clapped his hands together. "Now, that sounds like the first good idea of the day." Ray made his way to the West Side Highway and headed north.

"We leaving the city?" Donald asked.

"Yep."

"Where are we going?" Donald questioned.

Ray wasn't sure if Donald was wired up or not, so he had to be careful. "What do you got a million questions today? Relax and enjoy the ride."

Donald shrugged and leaned back in his seat. They drove for about forty minutes and got off at the Rye exit, a few miles north of the City in Westchester County. They drove for another ten minutes, and then Ray pulled onto a dirt road. They were in a heavily wooded area. They came to a sign that read 'Private Property.' Ray pulled into a long graveled driveway. He drove around the side of a huge house and parked in front of a barn.

When Ray shut the car off, Donald said, "Damn, we're in the middle of nowhere."

"Yep," Ray replied and got out of the car. Donald followed him out of the car and to the side of the barn. Jessie James, Cecil, and Apollo were there. They looked out of place in the woods in their nice city attire.

Apollo wasted no time with small talk. "Did they flip you yet, Donald?"

"What?" he asked, quite confused. Cecil came up behind him and ripped his shirt open. He was not wearing a wire.

"Apollo, what's going on?" Donald looked around the group, his nerves all of a sudden on high alert.

"You fucked up, Donald. You broke the rules. You sold dope out of the club."

Donald realized right away he was talking about Jerome. Did that double-crossing bastard go to Apollo? "I just needed a little extra cash, Apollo."

"We have rules for a reason, Donald. You don't have to understand them. You don't even have to agree with them - but you damn sure need to follow them. You didn't, and you sold to an agent. Jerome's an F.B.I.

agent, Donald. Sorry, my friend, but you're not leaving here. Make peace with your God if you have one."

Donald's eyes bulged out. "Apollo, I would never rat on you guys, you know that! Please, Apollo. What about my kids?" Donald got down on his knees. He began to shake all over; his teeth were chattering. He had no illusions about what was about to happen. "Please, Apollo. Give me a chance. I'll disappear. You'll never hear from me again."

Apollo looked at Jessie James and nodded. Jessie walked over to Donald and said, "You're going to disappear all right." He shot Donald once behind his ear. He was dead long before he hit the ground. Then Jesse James shot him two more times. They already had a hole dug in the woods. Cecil and Ray mixed up a batch of lye and a batch of cement. They dumped Donald in the hole and poured the lye on top of him. They waited thirty minutes and poured the cement into the hole. The last two feet they covered back up with dirt and then kicked leaves and branches all around it. A person could walk right by and never know there was a grave beneath the ground. They cleaned up and drove back to the city.

***

The ride to Little Rock from New York City took them almost two full days. The hit team took their time making sure they stayed under the speed limit the whole way. They had fake identification and guns in the trunk, so they had to be careful. Once they reached the Tunica casinos just on the other side of the Mississippi, Gino drove out to get them. This way, they wouldn't have to bring a car with New York plates into Little Rock. Gino had been changing hotels every day. He spent no more than one night in each place. By the time they got to the hotel room and talked about how they would handle Uncle Lenny, it was late Saturday afternoon.

"We go tonight as soon as it gets dark. It's a sleepy little town, so we can't go late. Let's rest up. We'll go in a couple of hours."

Max had just finished dinner when he realized that he had told Lenny he'd be there in the morning for breakfast. What the heck was he thinking? Tomorrow was Sunday, so he had to take the family to church and then breakfast. That was a tradition in the Hendrix home. He told his wife he had to run over to Lenny's but that he would be right back.

Lenny opened the front door, and the two men walked back to the kitchen. Lenny was drinking coffee as usual. "What's the matter? You had a fight with the little wifey?"

"No," Max laughed. "I forgot tomorrow's Sunday. We go to church and then to breakfast, so I can't come over in the morning." As an afterthought, he said, "Would you like to join us for church and breakfast?"

Lenny smiled and said, "No, Max. I don't think God wants me in His house.

" Max got real serious. "How could you say that? God loves you unconditionally."

Lenny got up. "Wait there. I'll be right back." He avoided the God conversation. Lenny went into his bedroom and grabbed a paper bag that was on the floor. He went back into the kitchen and placed the bag on the table.

"This is for you, Max. I want you to do something nice with your family. Take a vacation. There are fifty thousand dollars in there."

Max thought he was joking until he looked in the bag. "Oh my God, Lenny! It's full of money!"

Lenny looked at him like he was crazy. "I just told you that."

"Oh my Lord, where did you get this money?" Max asked.

Lenny waved his hand. "I've been saving it since before you were born. I've got plenty of money. I can't enjoy it, but I want you and your family to enjoy it. Max looked at the bills. They were all from the year two thousand two and up.

"Lenny, I might have been born at night, but not last night. What's going on with this money?"

"Didn't you ever hear the saying, don't look a gift horse in the mouth?"

"Of course, I have—but I can't accept this money, Lenny. What's the deal with this?" At that exact moment, three men burst in through the back door, catching Max and Lenny completely off-guard. Gino was first in, and he smiled when he saw Lenny.

"Hello, Lenny, how are you?" Lenny looked at Gino and the other two men. They looked familiar, but he didn't know them. Shit, what fucking bad luck having Max here. He'd have to try and convince them that they should let Max go. He pushed the bag into Max's hands and said, "Go now, Max. I'll talk to you tomorrow."

Gino wasn't having any of that. He put his silenced pistol into Max's ear and said, "Sit down, Max. You ain't going nowhere."

"Leave him, go." Lenny was about to say Gino's name but stopped himself. If he did that, they certainly wouldn't let him go, no doubt about it. "He ain't got nothing to do with this."

"He does now," Gino replied.

"He's a civilian. Don't get him involved."

"You already got him involved, Lenny." Gino took the bag and looked in it. "Ah, very nice. Where's the rest?"

"Let Max go, and I will take you to it."

Max wasn't exactly sure what was happening, but he knew it couldn't be good. He looked back and forth at the men and then looked at his friend. "Lenny, what's going on here?"

Lenny put himself in Gino's place. He knew if the shoe were on the other foot, he could never allow Max to leave. He'd consider him a casualty of war, and all's fair in love and war. Shit happens, even on sunny days. "I'm sorry, Max. Sorry I ever spoke to you. This here is Gino, and I don't know these other two, but I can assure you they're just as ruthless as Gino."

"Don't leave yourself out of that, Lenny. You're more ruthless than all of us together." Lenny ignored Gino and just looked at Max. "My name is not Mr. Rogers, Max. It's—"

Gino cut him off with laughter. "Mr. Rogers? Oh shit, Lenny, that's too fucking funny." Then he turned to Max and said, "His name's not important. What's important is that he ratted on his life-long friends, and to add injury to insult, he took about five million dollars of their money when he left."

Lenny shook his head. He knew it wasn't anything like five million, but what was the difference? By tomorrow, they would be calling it ten million. "Max, I wish I could get you out of this, but as you can see, I'm pretty helpless right about now."

Max was as scared as he could be. The monster of Spring Street may not be real, but that house was as haunted as any ghost could make it. "Gentlemen, this has nothing to do with me, so I'm leaving," Max said adamantly. He got up to leave, and Gino shot him in the temple. Max fell back onto the table and crashed to the floor. Ordinary Max died in a very unordinary way.

Lenny knew he was going to die, and truth be told, he really didn't give a crap, but this made him sick to his stomach. He put his hands over his face. "Oh shit, Gino, the guys got a wife and two little kids. He never did anything wrong in his life."

"Yeah, he did. He got hooked up with you," Gino said. "Now, where's the rest of the money?" "It's in the fucking closet."

Gino motioned for Charlie to go look. He came back a minute later with a zippered gym bag full of cash. Gino looked at it and said, "How much is here?"

Lenny shook his head. "I don't know, maybe a hundred thousand."

"Where's the rest, Lenny? Look, you ain't stupid. You know you're gonna die, but it can be a slow, painful death or nice and clean, quick and easy-like. Give up the money now, and it'll be painless, Lenny."

"Do whatever you want. There ain't no more money. I told Johnny. He knows. Johnny knows where the rest is. It ain't here."

Gino smiled. "You know what, Lenny? I believe you." And then, he shot Lenny in the head. They loaded the two bodies in the trunk of Lenny's car. Once they finished, they went back inside and cleaned up the blood. They broke the weapons down and wrapped them in a plastic bag. Gino kept a backup pistol just in case. Joey drove Lenny's car with Charlie. Gino followed in the rented car. They drove east for about an hour before they stopped at a truck stop. There was a young teenager there traveling west to Los Angeles, short on cash. The kid needed money for gas and food. Gino had him go inside and buy a gas can. When he came out, Gino gave him a hundred dollars and sent him on his way. They filled both cars up with gas as well as the gas can. They used the bogus credit cards Johnny had given them. Then they hit the road again. Another hour later, they were almost to the point where the New York car was left. Gino was glad to be out of Little Rock.

"Remind me to stay the fuck outta Elvis country. I don't know what these people do all day long. The fucking kid in the pizzeria didn't even know what a slice of pizza was. There ain't no real Italians in Little Rock. Get me home!" They found a wooded area off the main highway. They took the two bodies out of the trunk and put them in Lenny's car. The postmortem changes had begun, and rigor mortis had set in. It was difficult to move the bodies. They poured gas all over the two dead men and the car too. Gino stuck a rag in the gas tank and lit it on fire. They got back in the rental and drove off just as Lenny's car exploded in a ball of flames. Gino looked in the rearview mirror and watched the huge ball of black smoke rise into the sky. All he could think of was Home Sweet Home.

CHAPTER FORTY

The streets of Brighton Beach were hectic with Monday morning traffic. People were rushing to the trains to get to work. Merchants were opening up their shops. The sound of the ugly metal roll-up gates crashing open could be heard up and down the avenue. It sounded like an urban symphony of the start of a new day, money to be made. Boris took in the frantic scene with indifference from his warehouse office. None of that meant much to him as he looked out the window.

He was gloating from the report Stephan had brought him. He turned back around to face the men in the room. Ivan, Maxim, and Stephan were there waiting for his reply. "Tell me every detail again, Stephan. I want to make sure we're not missing anything."

"Not much to it, sir. Michael made contact with Little Mike. He was very happy and eager to hear from Michael. He said he had a shipment of coke that was for Russian Paul, and he needed to dump it. They are meeting tonight, and Little Mike will give the package to Michael on credit."

Boris thought for a moment. "It is not likely that Little Mike will deliver the package himself. Surely he'll have one of his men do that."

Stephan shook his head. "No, sir. Mike will bring it himself. He told Michael no one must know about this, not even his own guys. I think Little Mike is doing something he's not supposed to be doing, so he doesn't want anyone to know."

Boris looked at Ivan, who replied, "It's perfect." Looking at Maxim, Boris asked, "What do you think?"

"I think this whole thing is risky. Why not just leave it alone? You don't have to deal with him. Johnny has taken care of that."

Boris looked back to Stephan. "And your opinion?" Stephan thought for a moment. He quickly realized he was better off not taking sides. If he gave his opinion and things didn't work out, he'd get the blame.

"It is not my place to make decisions, sir. I just follow orders."

"It is your place, Stephan, to have an honest opinion. I am moving you up to join us at the top. You are a valued soldier, and your loyalty is unquestionable. You will now be in charge of all the troops like Ivan and Maxim. The four of us make the executive decisions for our Brotherhood. You three are my generals."

"Thank you, sir. I am honored."

"You're welcome. Now, what is your opinion?"

He thought for a moment again. "I feel confident in saying Little Mike is doing this on the sneak. He does not have the okay to do these kinds of deals, so, therefore, no one will know where he's going or what he's up to. He is a blood-sucking pig. I say we kill him."

Boris clapped his hands together and laughed. "Sorry, my friend," he said to Maxim. "You lose the vote, three to one." Boris turned back to Stephan. "This is what I want Michael to do," he said and began to outline the whole plan.

***

Mario was eating pistachio nuts while he talked to TD and the Conte brothers. They were in the 2nd Avenue diner in Manhattan. "Let's go over this one more time," he said.

"I'm going to drive you to the meet tomorrow morning," TD said. "This way, I can make sure everything is normal. After the meeting is over, I'll drop you a block away from where you have your car. Joe and Guy will be at Johnny's building waiting. As soon as I leave you, I join them."

Mario was nervous, and it showed. "I get that part. What I want to know is how you're going to snatch him off the streets?"

TD smiled. "I'm going to approach him as he goes into his building. I tell him there's a problem that we need to talk about. Once he gets into the car, it's over."

Mario wagged a finger at TD. "You see, that's not a solid plan. What if he tells you to take a walk, or he'll see you later?" "Then I pull my gun on him and make him get in the car." "And if he still doesn't do it, then what?" "I won't have much choice but to shoot him right then and there."

Mario shook his head. He didn't like that at all. Gunning down a captain in broad daylight would bring problems. This was killing Johnny Angel, not some nobody; it had to be perfect. "That's not a good move, Anthony."

"You got a better idea?" asked TD.

"What about doing it at nighttime?" asked Mario.

"There's no real pattern to where he goes at night. We'll be able to take him to his building. Don't worry, Mario. Leave that up to me. You know I never fail you."

Joe and Guy kept quiet during the whole conversation, but now Guy spoke up. "Mario, there's very little chance me and TD won't be able to get him in the car. Joey's gonna drive, so once TD approaches him, I can come up behind him. He won't be thinking he's gonna get whacked. He'll get in the car."

Mario laughed a nervous chuckle. "Let me explain something, kid. In this life, we're always thinking we're going to get whacked. That's second nature for us." Mario spat out a pistachio shell and nodded his head. "Okay, you guys sound sure of yourselves, so I'll trust you. So now you got him in the car, and then what?"

"Once he's in the car, I'll handcuff him so he can't do nothing stupid. We'll drive up to where the hole is and bury his ass. I'll have Joey and Guy drop me at my car, and I'll come and meet you at the Irishman's bar up in Van Cortlandt Park."

Mario snapped open another pistachio and ate it. There was something about this whole deal that was bugging him, but he couldn't put his finger on it. It was probably the fact that he was committing a cardinal sin and could easily die for it. But they were at the point of no return now, so he was all in. "I'm gonna be at my sister's house. It's five minutes away from the bar. Call me when you're there, and I'll meet you." Tomorrow afternoon, that little prick Johnny Angel should be sleeping with the angels.

**

Johnny liked spending Monday nights with Theresa and Angel watching Dancing with the Stars. He thought it was a good family show, and they all enjoyed it. When the show was over, he and Theresa tucked Angel in bed and went back to the living room. Maybe he'd just stay

345

home tonight. Johnny sat down on the couch, and Theresa came over and sat next to him.

"You going out?" she asked.

"No. I'll just relax with you tonight."

She was thrilled. "You want me to cook?" "Why don't you just order some Chinese." She went to call for Chinese food. Johnny sat thinking about his little family. Theresa was a good woman and sexy as hell. He enjoyed her and Angel's company. He wondered what it would be like to just take off and live the family life. He had more than enough money to last a lifetime. What more could a man want? He thought for a moment, and then he laughed. The thought was like a fish deciding to retire on dry land—impossible. Who was he fooling? He knew he could never live any life other than this one, the one that he chose. He never could understand how guys went to work every day, then back home, just to do it all over again tomorrow. The old saying on the streets, 'Guys in this life shouldn't get married,' was absolutely true for him, and he knew it.

Theresa came back in and sat down. "The food will be here right away." She noticed Johnny was deep in contemplation. "Penny for your thoughts?"

He snapped out of his thoughts and looked at her. "Sorry, honey, but my thoughts are a lot more expensive than that."

"Oh, really? And what do you think these are worth?" She took his hands and placed them on her breasts.

"Hmm, I'd say a dollar fifty."

She punched his shoulder. "A dollar fifty!"

"Each," he said, laughing. "A dollar fifty each." Johnny had his hands all over her breasts.

"Yeah," Theresa kidded. "Come and get your three dollars' worth then." She removed her top and undid her bra. He kissed her, and they started making love on the couch. They made their way to the bedroom for privacy in case Angel woke up. They had a quick but intense bit of sex, and as soon as they were through, the bell rang. The Chinese food had arrived.

***

The first thing Monday morning, Apollo woke to the ringing phone. It was Tonya, Donald's wife. She also called him yesterday when Donald did not come home Saturday night. Apollo told her he did not know where Donald was but not to worry about the club. He would send Jessie James to run things at the club until Donald showed up. Looking at the caller ID, he frowned. He dreaded the conversation but knew it was inevitable. "Hi Tonya, no word yet?" he asked with concern in his voice.

"No, Apollo. I'm really worried. He's been gone two nights without calling. He never does this. Not ever. Something is wrong."

Apollo felt bad for her, but there was nothing he could do. "Let me go ask around. I'm sure he's gambling or something. I'll call you later."

"Do you think I should call the police and file a missing person's report?" He sighed out loud.

"Well, Tonya, I don't want to tell you not to. But if you do, please keep my name out of it."

"Oh, of course. I would never bring you up. Apollo, you have helped our family so much over the years. I wouldn't dream of involving you."

"Thanks, Tonya. I appreciate that. You know Donald and I go way back. Just hang in there. He'll turn up sooner or later—and I'm going to kick him in the ass when he does show up."

She laughed. "Thanks for everything, Apollo."

"Bye, Tonya. I'll call you later." When he hung up, he felt like a big piece of crap. She made him feel so guilty. Oh well, as Johnny would say, this is the life we lead. He thought about the club. He hadn't been there in the last two nights. Jessie told him everyone was asking for Donald. Last night, Jerome had been pressing Jessie about Donald. Claimed he needed to talk with him badly.

Apollo decided to go there tonight and see what Jerome had to say. He spent the day doing paperwork at his office, and at three o'clock, he met Micki for lunch. "So, how's it going?" he asked her.

She looked a little worried. "Jerome is digging into me to find out about Donald. No one knows where he is. I'm scared, Apollo, but I feel better about everything now. I just couldn't do anything against you." Apollo was a little apprehensive about talking. He wasn't one hundred percent sure she was on his side. He was ninety-nine percent. He certainly wasn't ever going to concede the Donald deal to her, or anyone else for that matter. All of a sudden, he had a thought.

He smiled. "Marry me."

"What?" she asked, not thinking she heard him right.

"Marry me. Listen, I'm crazy about you, and I want to take care of you. Besides that, they can't make you testify against me if you're my wife."

"But they'll lock me up for sure, knowing I double-crossed them."

He shook his head. "No one needs to know we're married—at least not at this point."

"First of all, I have nothing I can testify about you anyway—and even if I did, I'd rather go to prison. I'd love to marry you, Apollo but not under these conditions. Let's wait this out."

"Okay, that makes sense. We'll just postpone the wedding. As for Donald, I don't know why he left, but someone told me he went to Jamaica. I have no idea what he's up to, but I'm sure I'll hear from him sooner or later." Apollo had gone to see Tonya before he met Micki. He had told her the same thing, so now the rumor would spread that Donald had left for Jamaica. Apollo thought he covered all his tracks pretty well. Johnny would be proud of him.

He took Micki back to his place once they were finished, and they made love the rest of the afternoon. He dropped her off at work and went inside for a while. He was sitting at the bar talking with Jessie when Jerome came over to him.

"Sorry to bother you, but can I have a word with you?"

"Sure," Apollo said. "How you doing?" They walked to the front entrance and outside to the sidewalk.

Jerome acted nervously. "I hope you don't mind me talking with you, but I've got a little situation. I was doing some things with Donald, and he's kind of disappeared, and now my deal is dying, and I stand to lose some money—and I was really counting on that money."

Apollo chose his words carefully. "Donald didn't disappear. I heard he's in Jamaica. What do you mean you were doing things with Donald? What things were you doing?"

Jerome looked around to make sure no one was too close. "I was moving coke for him."

Apollo acted surprised. "You were what?"

"I was moving coke, and I have a deal set up for tonight. That's why I wanted to talk to you. Do you think you can help me with that since he's not around?"

Apollo tried hard not to laugh. This fool thought he'd use Donald's absence to get close to him. "Jerome, I'm shocked that Donald would do such a thing. I can assure you I don't have anything to do with that kind of business, and you shouldn't either. You're Micki's brother, and I dig her, so I wanted to look out for you. That's why I got you a job here. You can make a decent dollar, and it's legit. Selling drugs is not a good idea, and I don't want you to talk about that anymore." He started to walk away and then turned back around. "Listen, Jerome, do you need a little loan to hold you over? I'd rather give you some cash than see you get mixed up in that shit."

"No, I'm okay. Thanks, Apollo."

"No problem." Apollo turned and walked to his car. He got in and drove away. He had a huge smile on his face. He couldn't wait to tell Johnny about this fool FBI agent. Johnny would definitely be proud of him.

CHAPTER FORTY-ONE

Tuesday morning was a bright, cloudless day. A slight wind kept the humidity from choking the world. Johnny got up and took a shower. When he came into the kitchen, Theresa had coffee and bagels ready for him downstairs. While he showered, she toasted a bagel and buttered it for him, placing it on a plate at his seat at the table. Johnny came downstairs and sat down, diving straight into the sports section. As he ate his bagel and drank his coffee, he glanced through the rest of the newspaper.

He stopped to read a story titled: Mobster Found Dead with Drugs. The story went on about Michael "Little Mike" DeStaffino, a soldier in the Lucchese Crime Family who was found shot to death in his car last night in Brooklyn. The article went on to say that the police searched the car and found a kilo of cocaine hidden in the trunk of the car. Apparently, it was a drug deal gone bad, according to the police. There were no suspects and no witnesses. The police were asking for help. They asked that if anyone saw anything, they should call the hotline number listed. Johnny put the paper down.

He immediately knew that Boris was behind this. That sneaky Russian! He wasn't really mad at him, but he needed to give him a hard time over this. After all, you just can't go around shooting Italians; especially made guys. Johnny was in a good mood, so he'd deal with Boris tomorrow. Angel joined him for breakfast. Theresa asked her, "You want cereal, or do you want me to make you pancakes?"

"I want a bagel, toasted with butter and coffee, please." Johnny looked over at her.

"Ain't you too young to have coffee?" Angel looked back at Johnny. As serious as she could be, she shook her head.

"No, Daddy, there isn't an age limit on the coffee can."

He laughed. "Okay, give the kid a little coffee."

Theresa said, "Eh, mami, I'll just give you a drop." "With milk and sugar, please!" she replied.

Johnny looked down at her. "Oh," he said, "you want coffee or tea?"

"Coffee, Daddy!" she said with a big smile. "Well, then you don't need milk and sugar."

"Please, Johnny," Theresa said. "The kid needs milk and sugar. If she drinks it black the way you do, she'll grow hair on her chest." Turning back to Angel, she said, "Here, mami, but hurry up! You're gonna be late for school." Angel finished her coffee and bagel, then kissed Johnny goodbye. Theresa kissed Johnny too, and the two of them left for Angel's school.

The apartment got real quiet. He sat there for a moment. It was nice having a family. He looked forward to watching Angel grow up and have children of her own. Yeah, he wanted to be around for that. He got up from the table and went upstairs to finish getting dressed. He had to be at the club in an hour for the Tuesday meeting with his crew. He knew today was going to be an interesting day.

When he walked into the clubhouse, Danny and Nick were playing gin. Johnny got a cup of coffee and watched his two old friends play. Danny picked a card, shuffled his hand around, and said, "Gin!" Nick counted his points, added the score, and said, "You win." Just for good measure, Nick threw the cards in the air.

"You must've fucking cheated, or you just got lucky!" Danny was laughing. "Call it what you want. The only important thing is whose pocket the money goes into. Ain't that right, Johnny Angel?"

"That's right," Johnny said, smiling. He was glad to see Danny win for once. "Pay the man, Nicky."

Sully walked in, looking dapper as always. "Hello, boys," he said. "Can a guy get a bet down here anywhere?"

"Not you," Nicky said. "The Schwartz boys still haven't gotten over that last move you made." Everyone laughed. Years ago, Sully found out where a lot of college football players hung out. He went to the bar and befriended them. He started buying beers and then shots. Sully spent four hours getting them wasted and the next day, bet twenty thousand with the Schwartz boys, three Jewish bookmakers. The team Sully bet was a long shot. Everyone knew it was going to be a blowout. It did turn out to be a blowout but not the way everyone thought. The team Sully bet won big that day, and Sully cleaned up. It turned out he had twenty grand bet with five different bookmakers for that game, and they still talk about it today, years later.

All the crew started showing up. Johnny hugged each man as they came inside. Mario came up to him and, with a big smile, hugged him and asked, "How's everything, Johnny?" concealing his true feelings well.

"It couldn't be better, Mario. Thanks for asking." Danny went around and spoke to everyone. When he was done, he and Johnny went outside for a walk. Like always, Johnny covered his mouth with his hand when he spoke, so if the Feds were watching, they couldn't read his lips.

"Any big deals?"

"Not really, just the usual bullshit. I'll handle it. Mario wants TD's name to be considered to get straightened out. What should I tell him?"

Johnny looked at Danny. "Tell him, I said over my dead body," and both men cracked up. "Tell Mario I said it would be a pleasure to put TD up for it. What else?"

"That's it for now."

"All right," Johnny said. "I gotta talk with Sully for a minute. See what he's doing with Sonny's guys." Both men went back inside the clubhouse. Mario was waiting for Danny, and after Danny spoke with him, he quickly left. TD was parked out front. When Mario got in the car, he said, "You're on, Anthony, make sure this works." TD drove a block away and dropped Mario off. "I'll call you when I'm on my way to the Irishman's place."

"We'll celebrate later," Mario said as he got out of the car."

"I'm looking forward to it, boss."

***

The Irishman's Pub was a bar on the upper west side of the Bronx, right on the Yonkers borderline. It was owned by Red Flattery. Red was an old Westies gangster. The Westies were a group of Irish gangsters from Hell's Kitchen. They belonged to the Gambino Family and were a wild bunch. Red ran a bookmaking and numbers operation out of the bar. He was a well-respected old-timer who had done a lot of work for the Italians.

TD called Mario about two hours after he left him. "I'm on my way there."

"Everything all right?" asked Mario.

"Exactly as it should be," TD answered.

"Great. I'll be there in ten minutes." Mario rushed over to the bar. When he walked in the front door, he saw TD sitting in the last booth near the kitchen entrance. He jumped in the booth and said, "So it's done?" he asked with a big smile on his face.

"Well, not exactly how you wanted it." TD answered, and then Johnny stepped out of the kitchen along with the Conte brothers, Danny and Nicky Black.

Johnny slid into the booth next to Mario and slung his arm around Mario's shoulder. He was all smiles. "Mario Mario Mario."

Mario turned white as a ghost. He pointed his finger at TD. "I don't know what this kid told you, Johnny, but he's a fucking trouble-making liar!"

"Really, and you proposed him to be straightened out this morning?"

There were a couple of guys sitting at the front table. Red politely asked them to leave. In this neighborhood—and this particular bar—no one asked questions. The men got up to leave. Red thanked them. A couple of guys at the bar were Red's guys. He locked the front door behind the last to leave and nodded to Danny.

"Mario, you fucked up. You know where your mistake was? When you told Anthony to kill the Conte brothers, you screwed up. Why should TD kill me and his buddies when he can just kill you? So, after he figured that out, he came to me. I actually had already told Danny I wanted to see him because you were acting real strange…" Pointing to the Conte brothers, Johnny continued, "These boys are good boys. Why would you want to kill them? I understand why you'd wanna kill me—but these two?" He looked over to Joe and Guy.

"Did you boys ever dig my hole?"

"Yes, sir, we did," replied Guy.

Johnny smiled. "My mother always says 'waste not, want not.' Take this piece of shit and put him in my grave. Only one thing, boys, don't kill him first. I want him buried alive. As the dirt is falling all over him, I want the panic to choke him as much as the lack of air." Johnny reached over and pulled Mario up and out of the booth by his ear. Mario yelled from the pain. When they were out of the booth, Johnny punched him square in the face. Mario went down, blood spurting from his nose.

Nicky helped him up just so he could knock him down himself. Danny walked over and kicked him in the ribs. Joey Conte moved in to strike next, but Johnny stopped him.

"Hold it, Joey. You can't hit a made guy." Everyone but Mario laughed. Johnny looked down at Mario. "Get to your feet before I step all over your head." Mario grabbed hold of the table and helped himself up. His face was bleeding, and he had peed his pants. He couldn't look any of them in the eye. "Mario, you're a disgrace to our thing, and I being your captain, formally strip you of your button. You're banished from our world, and you no longer have any privileges that come with that button." He looked over at Joey and smiled. "Joey, there's only three wise guys here," he said pointing to Mario, "ain't one of them."

Joey was a big boy at six feet four inches and weighing two hundred and fifty pounds. He grabbed Mario with his left hand and lifted him off his feet, and then punched him in the face with his right hand. Just as he hit Mario, he let go of him, and Mario literally went flying across the pub. Guy was completely different from his brother. He was six feet tall and weighed only one hundred sixty pounds. Guy and TD went over and kicked Mario, a bunch of times.

"That's enough," Johnny told them. "I want him alive when he goes in that hole." TD went into the kitchen and came out with a roll of duct tape. He tied Mario's hands behind his back and then taped his mouth shut. Joey Conte came over and picked Mario up like he was a heavy suitcase. He carried him out through the kitchen. They had their car parked right at the kitchen door. He popped the trunk and threw Mario in. He went back inside for further instructions.

Red's guys were already cleaning the blood up. "Anyone wants a drink?" he asked.

Danny laughed. "You fucking Irishmen drink on any occasion, don't you?" Red, who had a big red bubbly nose from a lifetime of heavy drinking, looked at him like he was crazy.

"We're in a bar, Danny. An Irish bar at that. People come here to drink. That's what they do here. Drink. Come, oh Danny Boy, oh Danny Boy, let me buy you a drink, oh Danny Boy!" He sang the words, and everyone laughed.

He took out a bottle of Sambuca from behind the bar and put it on the bar top. "Something I keep for my dear Italian friends." He then poured seven shots. He looked at TD and the Conte brothers and said, "I think a toast to choosing the right side is in order."

"Salute!" they all responded. Red poured another shot for everyone. "I think another toast is in order for all our friends we lost or who are locked up."

"Salute!" they all said. Red filled their glasses one more time and said, "Finally, I think another toast is in order." He smiled, and his nose seemed to light up the room.

"To Johnny Angel."

Made in the USA
Coppell, TX
13 November 2022

86288760R00203